# TAKING *My Life* BACK

# TAKING
## *My Life*
# BACK

My Story of Faith, Determination, and
Surviving the **Boston Marathon Bombing**

# REBEKAH
# GREGORY
### WITH **ANTHONY FLACCO**

**Revell**
*a division of Baker Publishing Group*
Grand Rapids, Michigan

© 2017 by Rebekah M. Gregory

Published by Revell
a division of Baker Publishing Group
P.O. Box 6287, Grand Rapids, MI 49516-6287
www.revellbooks.com

Printed in the United States of America

Library of Congress Cataloging-in-Publication Data is on file at the Library of Congress, Washington, DC.

978-0-8007-2821-2 (cloth)

978-0-8007-2866-3 (ITPE)

Some names and details have been changed to protect the privacy of the individuals involved.

Representation by Sharlene Martin of Martin Literary Management, www.MartinLit.com.

17  18  19  20  21  22  23      7  6  5  4  3  2  1

For Chris, Noah, and Ryleigh

You three are the reason I get out of bed
and put my leg on every morning.

# Contents

Contents

# Introduction

On April 15, 2013, the world came to know me as "Rebekah Gregory—Boston Marathon bombing victim."

I'd gone to Boston to cheer on a runner participating in the marathon. What should have been a day of celebration turned into the second largest terrorist attack on United States soil and the first time the American public heard of using pressure cookers to concentrate bomb blasts.

I almost died that day.

My son was sitting at my feet when the bomb went off behind me. My legs saved his life, and eventually I would lose my left leg despite valiant efforts to save it.

While my physical recovery is a credit to the excellent doctors and nurses who provided weeks and months of wonderful medical care, I believe with all my heart that I survived this traumatic experience to help others.

I have had many opportunities to tell my story of what happened that day, and people often share with me their own personal struggles with pain and loss. I'm always struck by how often we can relate to each other even though our circumstances vary.

———

Do I wish things were different? Every day. There is nothing I wouldn't give to have one more afternoon with my precious son before terrorism became part of our lives. But that is not possible. Instead, what is possible is to cherish the life God has blessed me with, because I have seen what it is like to almost lose it for good.

That is one of my main reasons for writing this book. It is less about my personal struggles and more about what each one has taught me: life is short. This is not just a cliché. It was not until a bomb shattered my world that I realized I had been doing everything wrong.

These chapters were painful to write. Even my closest friends don't know some of the details. So, if you expect to read about a perfect Christian life with a pretty little bow on it, you have picked up the wrong memoir. What you will read about is someone who tries to live the Christian life, who tries to walk with God, and who has not always succeeded in getting things right.

Life is messy and complicated. Things happen every day that can cause us to lose sight of our joy. Yet we were never promised a life without hardship. I have learned that firsthand. And I can tell you that every obstacle I have experienced and decision I have made have helped me become a stronger person.

Who knows—if my story would've started the day of the bombing, my feelings might not be the same. But it didn't. And looking back now, at every obstacle I have encountered prior to April 15, 2013, I wonder if I was being prepared to tackle the biggest one of all just a little bit better.

While we cannot predict what will happen to us or if a bomb will go off at a marathon we are attending, I believe we can take comfort that God is in control.

In the media, I'm often referred to as a victim of the Boston Marathon bombing. I am not a victim. I refuse to see myself as a victim.

I am a survivor.

This is the story of how I took my life back.

*Part One*

# BOMBS *and* HOSPITALS

# –1–

# Grim Reapers
# and Their Cooking Pots

On April 15, 2013, the crowds who swamped the finish line for the Boston Marathon repeated a tradition that had taken place for the past 116 years. We took pride in attending the world's oldest annual marathon, a public celebration of exertion and stamina.

The weather was clear and perfect, but several hours had passed since the race began. Boredom and anxiety mixed for the spectators while people bunched near the finish to see their friends and relatives cross the line.

We were three hours and forty-eight minutes into the race, and the top runners had long since finished. The best of them had been done long enough to get back to their hotels or homes and be soaking in the Jacuzzi.

Nevertheless, the finish line area along Boylston Street was packed, and there were over five thousand runners still out on the course. Spectators who remained at the finish were there because they knew at least one of the runners yet to come in and appreciated how hard they were working to make the distance.

It was my birthday weekend and my first time in Boston. I was there with my five-year-old son, Noah, and a guy I had been casually dating. His mother was running in the race and was due at the finish line any minute. The presence of so many inspired runners filled the air with a contagious feeling of hope. The celebrations at the finish created a sense of community that we all seemed to feel.

But not everyone felt that way.

It was 2:49 in the afternoon. Noah had started out the day enthused to be at the race, but at his age he soon grew tired of waiting for the runners to finish streaming by. So I set him down on the sidewalk at my feet, with his back resting against my shins.

We were both in that position when the first bomb went off.

The blast wave hit like a freight train and I felt as if the street itself had exploded.

All of a sudden I found myself thrown back, sprawled on the ground, like something out of a movie. *What? What just happened?* Somehow I wasn't knocked out, but the power of the blast flattened me so hard and fast that it had me in a world of its own. A deafening clang reverberated in my head.

Smoke filled the air. I tried to move, but my limbs felt paralyzed.

The Boylston Street sidewalk was now a canvas for the widespread scattering of blood and bones.

Breezes stirred the smoke into isolated wisps. I managed to slightly lift my head, enough to see my body covered in blood. Bits of flesh, including pieces of my own leg bones, were plastered all around me. I raised my gaze a little higher and saw other victims. There was no telling how many.

Wide streaks of crimson showed in every direction. Pieces of metal were scattered everywhere. Random body parts were strewn among the bodies themselves.

The entire finish line was no longer recognizable. We were in a war zone. But as horrific as that scene was, my true nightmare came a few moments later when my mind cleared enough to remember that Noah had been sitting on my feet with his back against my legs.

Now my legs were shredded and I couldn't see my son anywhere.

———

I tried to scream for someone to find him, but I could barely hear myself or anything else over the gong reverberating in my head. Then a few moments after the first explosion (I didn't know until later that the interval was twelve seconds), the second bomb went off. It didn't seem to be that far from us, and it nailed down the certainty that this was some sort of deliberate attack. Now the pandemonium was thick. Panicked bystanders and baffled officials struggled to respond.

From the corners of my limited field of vision I saw the yellow jackets of race officials swarming the scene, joined by a few of the spectators. Some of those who had escaped injury were attempting to provide first aid or perhaps comfort the dying.

I felt as if I were being torn apart by a predator. It was more than my mind could process. I mustered any physical strength that was left in me and tried to scream again for my son, for Noah, but everyone within earshot was either injured, stunned, or preoccupied with first aid and essential medical help.

At that point my initial shock subsided enough for the pain to come roaring in. It was paralyzing, unlike anything I've known. The pain also made it clear that this thing might have already killed me. My instincts seemed convinced that I would be pulled down the same road as the nearby silent victims unless I fought back. I struggled to comprehend.

*Where's Noah? We're hurt. Where's Noah? An explosion. He was sitting against my legs. Where's Noah?*

I was helpless. Smoke kept getting in my eyes, making it hard to see.

An instinctive force compelled me to find Noah and start taking care of things, but at the same time I realized this was a futile impulse. My muscles and bones couldn't obey. Trying harder didn't help. All of a sudden my entire body was the wrong tool for the job.

At that point, that very instant, I felt the way I had when I was a little girl. It was like running into a bully you haven't seen in years. My memory flashed fear and outrage from a time when I had no power to change my circumstances and could escape only by retreating into a fantasy world.

But on this day, in the aftermath of the explosion, my lifelong skill at distancing myself from turmoil was useless. The reason was Noah. My love for him nailed me to the present moment and to the loathsome power of the facts that my legs were destroyed and my little boy had vanished from my sight.

The smell of the explosives lingered, and the sounds of panic filled the air—the screams of injured blast victims and the screams of their loved ones. Over the ringing in my head, those screams were tiny and faint.

None of us who were conscious knew anything about terrorism yet, only that something had exploded behind us. Inside the carnage, its cause didn't matter.

The thought of Noah also being a victim of this thing hurt like taking a spear to the chest. Instinct kept telling me I was in danger of bleeding out, but I didn't want to know anything else except what had happened to him. The prospect of leaving this world before I could do anything to help him was unbearable. I'm certain every parent feels something similar for their child in dire circumstances. I had to know what had happened to him. No matter what the truth was, I had to know.

My eardrums felt as if they had been blown out by the blast (and it turned out they had). The gong still reverberated deep in my skull and threw up a din that drowned out nearly everything else. The throbbing pain was matched by the burning stabs from the shrapnel punctures all over my body. Shrapnel also covered everything else around me, as if a cloud of metallic insects had died in flight and fallen straight to the ground.

By the time I noticed my clothing was also smoldering, one of the first responders had already run over and began pulling the burning clothes away from me. All I remember is that he was male.

He put his forehead next to mine and shouted loudly enough for me to hear him, assuring me I would be taken care of. I couldn't make coherent responses, but I understood he was there to give me a chance at life.

He was doing this even though the second explosion had made it plain nobody was safe. For all he knew, a third bomb and a fourth bomb were about to go off, taking him out along with me.

He should have run for his life. Instead, he became my visiting angel.

I remember lying back and looking up at the sky. I said a silent prayer: *God, if this is it for me, take me, but let me know my son is okay.*

---

I want to warn skeptical readers in advance that I can't explain what happened next. But while I lay there, barely able to see, barely able to hear, I got the distinct impression of Noah's voice hollering, "Mommy! Mommy!" from somewhere close behind me. I couldn't see him and I shouldn't have been able to hear him. The ringing in my head covered all but the loudest sounds.

But his voice was clear to me. (In video of the event, he can be heard calling out to me.) The explosion had left me on the street at an angle, and I was able to twist my head to see him on the ground a few yards behind me. I couldn't tell how injured he was. Since my legs were useless, my first reaction was to stretch out my arms to pull him toward me, even though he was too far away for that to be possible. The feeling of fire blazing in my left arm caused me to glance at it while I attempted to reach out. For the first time, I saw that my left hand was shattered, with bones sticking in all directions. The skin had peeled back all the way to my wrist.

Noah was right there, but I was unable to pull him to me and embrace him. Now, as much as the physical pain, it was frustration that fueled my agony.

My friend's aunt was nearby, unhurt. She and some first responders picked Noah up and began to tend to him. Videos of the scene show him in the arms of a police officer, although I missed seeing that happen. Amazingly, he hadn't been badly injured. There was very little blood, and he wasn't burned. His leg was bleeding, but it appeared he wasn't damaged anywhere near the extent that I was.

And at that point Noah's safety was all that mattered. It made no sense to me that he was so free from injury, but gratitude filled my heart anyway. I call it a Jesus moment, because even though my body was on fire, my terror for my child eased. *Noah was alive.*

Out there on that street, I felt my priorities shift the instant Noah's survival was confirmed; I could let my own condition become important. Surviving became my goal. My first question was the same as it would be for any other single mother: *Who will take care of my child if I'm not here?*

Unless I could somehow rally, my son would have been spared from the explosion only to watch me die on that pavement. My gratitude for his survival was muted by my wondering what it would do to him if I succumbed out there. My sense of helplessness became a force as great as my physical pain.

Time broke into pieces after that, like a sketch artist flipping through a stack of progressive drawings. I lay there for what felt like forever. The whole time my body burned with pain that was amplified by my panic. They blended together and became a fearsome thing.

An emergency medical technician leaped from an ambulance that was suddenly close by. I could faintly hear him shouting right next to me, "We need to get her off the street or she'll die here!" I was only vaguely aware that he was referring to me.

I felt myself lifted onto a gurney, and the movement woke up every nerve cell in my body. None of us knew if more carnage was still to come, but professional first responders, as well as brave Good Samaritans, were all around me, moving fast and with determination. They are the reason I am still here to tell you this.

However, even in rescue, my sense of helplessness persisted. I had no choice but to relax into their care. There was far too much to deal with on my own. The pain was too much. The fear of dying before I saw Noah again was far too much. At the rate I was bleeding, I had only a few minutes left.

I felt them load me into the ambulance, locking me down and checking my vitals. I tried to get them to look at my hand. Instead they seemed a lot more concerned with my overall condition. We all knew it was bad.

I glanced up at the guy who had loaded me into the ambulance just in time to see him yell to the driver, "We have an amputee . . ." His voice barely penetrated the ringing in my ears, but I read his lips and was alert enough to understand him. Even if I survived, life as I knew it was over. I didn't take that thought any further, though. I couldn't.

We pulled away in the ambulance and reality started fading in and out. I begged them to put me to sleep, but instead they kept shaking me to keep me awake. In my confusion, their kindness felt cruel.

I remained conscious throughout the ambulance ride. I'm certain it was only an illusion that the driver aimed for every pothole that came along. Nevertheless, by the time we got to the hospital, the jostling had lifted my pain level to an obscene degree. It was a complete assault on my senses.

The doctors gave me a quick look and immediately called out to prep me for surgery. Just before they began to administer the anesthetic, a lady came in and asked me if there was anyone she could call for me. I tried over and over to get my mother's number out. It was ridiculously hard to pronounce . . . those . . . few . . . digits.

When she finally got it all down, that was it for me. My strength was down to the dregs. At last they pumped me full of medicine, and the anesthesia helped me to melt out from under the pain.

Whether or not my surgeons already knew about this new tactic of using pressure cookers to magnify blast pressure, I later learned they could tell by the pattern of damage across my body that I had been only a few feet away from the sidewalk blast. They did their best to repair me on the operating table and made valiant efforts to save both of my legs and to give me back a left hand that might be functional one day.

The challenges they faced turned out to be too much, despite their depth of skill. They could save my life, but my legs were so ruinously shredded that it was doubtful both could be saved. Even if they could be repaired to some degree, it would require numerous surgeries over time. As for my general injuries, my body was riddled with bits of bomb shrapnel. The nails, nuts, and bolts packed in the bombs that hadn't landed on the street had ended up inside everyone within range. Some of the bits that tore into my flesh could be teased back out through weeks of surgeries, but to this day I still carry others in places where their retrieval is too risky to justify yet another operation.

I had no sense of time. I had simply felt the doctors and the operating room drift away. I passed through a weird form of nothingness . . . and then opened my eyes again.

# -2-

# Arms of Love
# and the Terrorist
# Down the Hall

It felt like only a few minutes had passed, as if I had nodded off for a quick nap. But the first person I saw when I opened my eyes was my mother. This was strange, since I was in Boston and she lived in Texas. But it was such a relief to see her that I didn't worry about the time jump. There she was, escorting me into the world for a second time.

There was a breathing tube down my throat, which left me no way to talk. Mom began by softly assuring me that she loved me and she would stay with me, and then she explained that she was in Boston because someone had set off bombs at the marathon but that I was going to survive this and so was Noah. She told me that in the confusion after the attacks, he had been taken to a different hospital, Boston

Medical, but he was expected to make a full recovery and be released soon.

On the day of the attacks, Mom and Dad had been in the process of moving into a new house in Houston. They were at Home Depot when they got the call from the hospital. The nurse only told them that I had an "ankle injury." But when they asked to speak with me and were told I was in the ICU, they knew the news was much worse than that.

They scrambled to pick up Allie, my youngest sister, from school and place her with a friend, and then they hurried off to fight rush-hour traffic and make the last flight to Boston. Dad planned to stay with Noah at Boston Medical, where he would remain for a few days since there was no medical reason to move him to my hospital. It was already packed with its share of the more than two hundred victims.

When I say my dad was staying with Noah, I am referring to Tim Gregory, the wonderful guy Mom married three years after she and my biological father divorced. Tim adopted my two sisters and me the following year, when I was fourteen, and gave me an authentic experience of a father's love. Later they had their daughter Alexandria, whom we call Allie, who was waiting back in Houston. Tim taught me that it isn't a father's biology that matters; it's the depth of his concern and his steadfast presence.

While he planned on staying with Noah, Mom was determined to remain with me around the clock. Noah had been sedated and was sleeping when they first got to town, so Dad had insisted on coming with her to see me before he went to be with Noah.

I kept gesturing toward my legs, which I couldn't see. The pain made it feel as if they were both gone. I couldn't lift myself up enough to look, and Mom couldn't convince me they were there. She finally used her phone to take a photo of them and showed me the remains of my legs to assure me I still had them for the time being.

Her plan sort of worked. There was the photo, clear enough, and apparently those two masses of torn and stapled flesh were my legs. What I didn't know yet was that my legs, as I knew them, existed now only in the old normal.

The old normal was in the past. The old normal had blown away on that first bomb's blast wave. Of course, with the old normal gone, that would seem to imply a new normal was lurking around nearby. Lying there, I had no idea what this new normal could possibly be. Surely it looked better than those two masses of what were supposed to be my legs.

The main power of that photo was to reveal the stark truth about my son's survival. Everything embedded in me would have been inflicted on Noah if my legs and torso hadn't been between him and the bomb. So the injuries in Mom's photo were a mirror image of what would have been done to his little body. Right where my shredded legs took so much of the blast was where his back and his head would have been directly exposed.

At that moment, lying there in that hospital bed, the first real awareness of my overall situation came to me. It was terrifying, to say the least, but I was thankful that Mom and Dad were there to surround me with their love once again. I could feel the beauty of it even above the pain. And as I look back on it now, it's also clear that my true journey of recovery began at that moment.

I had survived. Noah was going to be okay. For us, the Grim Reaper had slipped out of the room and moved on. But

I would find out that an eight-year-old boy named Martin Richards had been killed, and his mother and seven-year-old sister were fighting to recover. Several other people had also been killed and hundreds more injured. Some were struggling to overcome their injuries right there with me on the same floor at that same moment. It seems to me that the sum total of pain and fear in Boston's hospital wards during those days can never be fathomed.

I didn't have to know their names to feel for them. Many, like me, had nearly died but became survivors when they felt just enough strength returning to keep them in their body and in this world. No doubt every one of us was doing our own version of wondering how we could cope with this and go back to living.

I was mostly out of it for the next three or four days, with additional surgeries and strong pain medication. It was only on Saturday, five days after the explosions, that I was lucid enough for Mom to let me know that Noah had been released from the hospital and that he and Dad would soon be at my bedside for a visit. I could have screamed with delight if I had the power. Instead, I sighed with deep relief.

This felt like a repeat of the first thoughts my mom and I had shared when I briefly woke up the first time. After I had tried a little sign language, with poor results, Mom found some paper and a pencil. She gave them to me, and I used my undamaged right hand to write my first words in shaky letters: *God is not finished with me yet.*

After that I scrawled, *Angels were all around us.*

Mom still has that note.

28

During the first three days, while I was in a state that amounted to a chemically induced coma, my left leg had been fitted with an external device called a fixator. This is a lightweight steel frame that surrounds the leg. For the next two days, after I woke up, I was still out much of the time. But after that it was time to deal with recovering while awake. Talk about fun! A fixator is attached by long screws that penetrate the flesh and continue into the bone. My remaining leg bones were so shattered that the fixator was needed simply to hold them in place. I had been warned that it would take months to know if the device had been effective. Boy, when you listen to news like that while metal pins are burrowed through your muscles and into your bones, it darkens your view of the immediate future. Your only choice is to play the long game.

Mom got permission to set up a cot next to my bed, and even though the room was deliberately kept very cold because the pain medication I was on made me so hot, she wouldn't leave me. I was in that hospital room for thirty-nine days before being transferred to Houston for an additional seventeen days of hospitalization, and she stayed the whole time.

At first, she kept a hotel room as a place to store her things, change clothes, and grab a shower, although most of the time she used the shower in my room. She seldom left my side, and throughout my stay I repeatedly witnessed how vital it is to have a personal advocate when you are incapacitated. They can be lifesavers, even in simple ways such as insisting that no one touches you without using fresh gloves or washing their hands in your presence before doing so. Once, when a staff member was bending over me to adjust my pillows under my legs, she bumped the fixator and a wave of pain shot through my entire body. My mother then decreed that nobody would adjust my pillows but her. Thank you, Mom.

I was grateful for my own survival and especially for Noah and his good condition, but I had a hard time maintaining my gratitude. My level of pain was too severe. The fixator rods felt like rows of knife blades penetrating my flesh. I was kept on a cocktail of pain meds and antibiotics, but the goal was for me to remain as awake as I could while still having some pain relief. It would have been too dangerous to keep me under for as long as the device was in place.

I can say that throughout that hospital ward, the staff all seemed to have an extra measure of seriousness about their duties and concern for their patients. This attack, after all, had happened in their hometown. Some of them may have known one or more of the victims, since there were hundreds, and they were now working in packed conditions because of the sudden flood of the injured. I could tell by their remarks that this thing was intensely personal to all of them.

For me, this provided a degree of emotional relief, because they felt themselves to be in the same boat with us. Their need for us to recover was partly born of their own need to do whatever was possible to set things right.

On day five after the attack, two FBI agents in dark suits arrived at my bedside. It felt as if someone else's movie had been spliced into my life.

They apologized for approaching me so soon but told me I was a victim of an organized terror attack and that nobody knew how many more attackers might still be out there. They told me one attacker had been killed trying to evade capture early in the morning of day four and that his younger brother had been caught after a shootout late that night. He had been shot several times but was alive and in custody.

Then they informed me that the surviving Boston bomber was, at that very moment (take a deep breath with me here . . .), a patient in this same hospital. Right there on my floor.

Students of irony will savor that one; the stranger who had killed several innocent people and shredded hundreds more—some with grotesque losses of limbs—was now under medical care just down the hall from my room and the rooms of many of his other victims. I instantly gained new appreciation for what people mean when they use the phrase, "you can't make this stuff up."

Intellectually, I understood. Nobody needed to explain to me that the injured suspect had the right to be restored to some degree of health before being put on trial. I didn't have to be told that his bullet wounds were likely similar to the shrapnel wounds so many of us suffered from, and therefore it was logical for him to be treated here because of the high quality and experience levels of the doctors and staff. I got it. I knew.

Still. A perpetrator whose deliberate actions had caused so much heartache to peaceful strangers was being tended to by some of the same people helping me. I could walk down the hall and look him in the face, if I still had legs that worked.

So the devil was in the house. Boy, did that news ever cast a pall over the room. The air began to feel hot and stuffy. I already had a fever, courtesy of all the inflamed and infected injury sites, and with this intensely frustrating news my temperature seemed to spike.

Along with a deep feeling of anxiety came a strong impulse to get up and move, pace the room, walk the halls, run out of the building with my mom in tow, and—even though the new normal made it impossible—grab Noah and take us all back home to Texas.

The impulse strengthened, became a yearning to put as much distance as I possibly could between me and my family and the killer who had brought so much evil to this city and who was now only a few yards away.

It took concentrated effort to stay focused and maintain a conversation with the agents. Somehow the news made my physical pain worse. And right then, everything hurt. Large areas of my legs were covered with wide bands of stitches. Several inches of the fibula bone had been blown away from my left leg. The surgeons had taken strips of skin off of my outer left thigh to cover blast holes in my lower leg.

I had missed the killer's arrival to the hospital because I had mostly slept through the day before, when the police had brought him in. I later learned they had completely locked down the hospital for the day in order to stabilize the security situation. My mom was caught outside for many hours and couldn't get past the guards. By the time I awoke on Saturday, she had been admitted back in. Now she hovered protectively while the men questioned me.

It didn't take long for the agents to realize I didn't have much information, although one of the bombers must have passed within a few feet of me when he placed the bomb on the ground behind us. The agents let me know I would likely have more visits with them as time went on. Then they moved on to the next victim. They had their work cut out for them. With so many victims in the hospitals to see, the agents were going to be around for a long time.

As for me, their questions told me a lot about the attacks and caused a strong sense-memory to overcome me. In it, I was a freshman in high school, sitting in business management class and watching the horror of the 9/11 attacks in New York City. And while this attack in Boston was smaller, that made no difference to the dead and wounded. It was cut from the same bloody cloth.

———

With the FBI agents gone and the brutal reality of this thing sinking in, I cried for all of us—for Noah, for my mom and dad, for every living soul in range of those cowardly devices. I felt overwhelmed with grief for the dead, for their families, and for the injured children most of all. They had been introduced to far too much of the world's evil too early in life.

Noah's relatively mild injuries made him among the luckiest kids out there that day. Yes, this is a surreal definition of the word *luck*, but I was glad enough to take it.

However, then as now, I don't know why God spared us. I honestly have felt a deep sense of guilt wash over me many times. It was certainly not that we were recipients of grace because we deserved it more than others. I have never been comfortable with any implication that, in a situation such as this, the worst victims are somehow less favored by the Lord.

Before the explosions, the marathon had seemed to threaten nothing worse than blisters and pulled muscles. It hadn't even occurred to me to pray for our safety that day or for the safety of thousands of spectators and runners. I suppose the greatest impact of terror is that it is unexpected.

---

Mom often prayed with me in the hospital. The shared devotion time was a deep bonding experience for us. Despair was scratching hard at my door. Life had become one big waiting game and any type of future was so uncertain.

During those times, we often referenced a song called "Help Me Find It," by the Sidewalk Prophets. In the song they talk about being still for the moment and the importance of letting God take the lead. Being still was one of the hardest things for me to accept. Before the marathon, my life had been nonstop. For me, it was like I went from going a hundred miles an hour to screeching to a complete halt. And because of this, I would often find myself listening to this song over and over. But as hard as everything was, its powerful words gave me an important reminder: no matter what was in store, I would never have to face it alone.

I truly do believe that. After all, my son, Noah, is a living, breathing example that miracles do exist. Who am I to question anything else? I have learned to be grateful for even the smallest of victories. Gratitude became an enduring attitude for me at the moment my mom and dad arrived to stand up for me and my precious son, bearing the news that Noah had survived and would recover and that they were there for me.

# -3-

# Piece by Piece

Noah was in his hospital bed for five days before my dad could take him out of there and bring him to the hotel. On the sixth day, after I had been out of my drug-induced unconsciousness for twenty-four hours and had a chance to clear my head of the anesthetics, Dad brought him to see me.

I felt strangely nervous ahead of the visit, wondering if my injuries would upset him. Mom helped me prepare as well as we could, putting my dingy "hospital hair" in a ponytail and covering the gruesome device on my left leg with a blanket. I sat up in bed and prepared my best mom smile, so eager to see my son again.

I already knew the blast had left Noah with a bone-deep gash in his right calf, which was all stitched up but much too sore for walking on. But the surprise was that he arrived in a little red wagon Dad had bought for the purpose. He pulled it into the room with Noah riding in it. Noah's eyes lit up the moment he saw me, and instantly my anxieties disappeared.

Better yet, in spite of my worries over the impact my injuries might have on him, at first he showed no reaction to them at all. He was just overjoyed to see his mom.

As for me, I was flabbergasted. As if the moment wasn't already perfect, Noah was so excited that he got up out of the wagon in spite of his row of painful stitches (and oh, could I empathize) and stepped over to my bedside.

I have never had a more welcome hug or felt more grateful to receive one. To be allowed to return to life with my little boy was beautiful beyond description. To have him there in my arms, knowing we had a future together—at least some sort of future together—was perfection. It made no difference that I was at a loss as to how to begin working it out. All I could think was, *I'll take it.*

Noah wore a distinctive blue FBI jacket, which Dad explained had been given to him while they were on their way to see me. They ran into an FBI agent waiting at the elevator and quickly learned he was one of the guys who had caught the other bomber. He was on the floor because of the new resident down the hall. When he learned that Noah was one of that bomber's victims, he gave him his jacket as a sign of brotherhood. This made the jacket too cool for words, and Noah beamed in it.

---

I had worried about how to talk to Noah about what had happened to us, but since there was no way to sugarcoat it without some ridiculous fiction, I decided to just keep it simple. Give it a name. Give him a way to talk about it, if he wanted to, but not try to force anything out of him. Let the rest work out in its own time.

I knew he had to have picked up a story of some kind, although Dad said he hadn't shown much curiosity about it. But I also knew he would look to me to describe this thing for him. The picture we made of it together would form his way of remembering it and of thinking about it far into the future. Like drawing a design in wet concrete, it was important to give him an image he could use before everything hardened.

We talked about how there had been two bad men who set off two bombs and hurt a lot of people they didn't even know, but the police had caught them and now they couldn't hurt anybody else anymore. Noah seemed fine with that description and didn't express any curiosity to know more about the men or their motives. *Bad men do bad things.* He got it.

Noah and Dad stayed for a couple of hours, and in that time the procession of nurses and doctors kept on moving through the room and the daily treatments continued. When Noah overheard the staff members talking about how much weight I'd already lost, with repeated surgeries yet to come, he grabbed my untouched meal tray and insisted on spoon-feeding me the dish of Jell-O. My appetite was laid flat by the antibiotics, surgical anesthesia, and daily pain meds. I couldn't do much more than swallow water.

Still, it turned out that Noah and I both needed the experience he was offering. He was gaining the assurance of helping his mom get better, and for me, I realized how much better the food tasted from his spoon. I ate the entire bowl. I tell you, lying there in that hospital bed, with him there next to me, serving me, was as holy and wonderful an experience as anything I have ever known.

The doctors had placed my damaged left hand in a large splint, which helpfully concealed the injury. Noah was adamant about signing his name on it. He was so proud to have recently learned how to form those four letters, and he carefully wrote them down with a serious sense of purpose.

It was the best gift I could have ever received. A sample of Noah's first handwriting was going to be right there in front of my eyes for as long as the splint remained.

And from that moment, it was as if the letters he carefully printed contained so much of his innocent love in them that they radiated power. They didn't stop the physical pain, but suddenly I felt more strength to endure it. My gratitude for the gift of his little signature overflowed.

I chose the name Noah for my son because I love the biblical reference in the Old Testament to the humility of Noah and to his great accomplishment. I consider it one of many blessings that my little boy has either rescued me from my own floods or given me reason to swim harder, time and time again. Then and now, my Noah keeps me inspired.

His visit that day went by too quickly, but I felt my energy draining away. When Dad saw that the time was right, he took Noah back to the hotel. Soon they would fly back home to Houston while my recovery continued in Boston.

Part of my joy of the day was seeing Noah lifted up by his visit. His beaming smile and happy energy were a relief for both of us. He had been stuck for five days in a room full of strangers, watched over by his loving grandaddy but still without his mom's presence, enduring painful medical procedures. I don't remember being five years old, but my memories begin a year or two later, and I clearly recall how long a week was back then. No wonder he was so visibly relieved.

My heart felt like a helium balloon that had just drifted up to the ceiling.

—

My mom was my connection to the outside world. One of the most important things she did for me was control what was kept out of my room, such as news of further miseries we could do nothing about. Her goal was to maintain a positive healing environment as far as the situation would allow. Now I can look back on it and see how wise that was.

During the hospital stay I continued to drop weight fast. Since I was already pretty slim when the attacks occurred, it was more than I could safely lose. It turns out that repeated surgeries are a very effective weight loss program. I was locked into a series of operations that had to be scheduled nearly every other day, with a day or so between each for recovery and to get most of the anesthesia out of my system before starting again.

I couldn't eat after midnight on any day when I was scheduled for surgery the next day, and coming out of anesthesia I had no appetite. The next day I was free to eat if I could—but only until midnight, since there would be another surgery after that recovery day. During the recovery day, either the pain made food unappealing or the pain-relieving drugs again blocked my appetite. Move over, Weight Watchers.

With Noah back in Houston so he could return to school and so Dad could return to work, I was humbled by Dad's quiet resolve and loving support. I was so grateful to know that Noah was safe with him, giving me the time and space to recover. My son had come so close to being taken out by that explosion, underlining his preciousness to me, which was reemphasized when the doctors told me I had taken so much internal damage from the tiny shrapnel bits that I was unlikely to be able to conceive a child again or to carry one to term. Another kiss on the cheek from the terrorists.

This was the life I had awakened to discover after the bombing, and my days consisted of being gradually pieced back together, day after day after day. The doctors were still trying to save my left leg, damaged far worse than my right, but a lot of the surgeries concentrated on a term I had never heard before: *debridement*. And no, debridement is not the process a man goes through to divorce his wife; it involves removing foreign objects from living tissue to minimize infection and inflammation. Debridement. Debriding. Debride. I could have gone a lifetime without learning those words.

They couldn't debride the shrapnel bits out of me all at once. There were far too many. In some places, my flesh was so impregnated with debris that an X-ray looked like sprinkles suspended in Jell-O. Bits of metal and plastic were all through my thighs, back, and calves. The surgeons concentrated on getting the big pieces, but there were so many small ones that in order to remove them all they would have had to carve me up until my flesh was shredded.

For that reason, the debriding process went on for weeks. During those first few weeks, I was wheeled into surgery eleven times, with multiple surgeries performed under each session of anesthesia, followed by a rest day, for a total of dozens of operations. From the beginning, those days were a constant routine of cleaning the open wounds and changing dressings, removing stitches and putting in more.

The pain never got better, although I was clearheaded enough to realize that its levels were far less than I would have felt without the meds. I couldn't move either leg at first. On the left leg, half of the fibula and many of the bones in the foot were all gone, just blown away, requiring the steel fixator. My right side had been ripped open by shrapnel and had stitches everywhere.

Any movement caused the pain to flare. I tried to find a position that might allow me any comfort at all, and Mom was endlessly patient in adding and subtracting the pillows under my legs. When we found a position that worked, it brought a few minutes of relief, but the pain always found me and crept back in.

A particularly kind resident observed that I had hundreds of stitches that had to be removed and restitched every time a surgery affected the areas, and she took over that challenge. So after she did her required rounds one day, she came in on her own time and carefully removed each stitch, one by one, and gently cleaned the wounds. There was no way to eliminate the pain of it, but her smooth and careful hands worked with such accuracy that she barely disturbed the flesh around each stitch as she cut it and pulled it out.

It took over an hour for her to carefully remove each one. It allowed me the least painful process that could be had, and at the same time it showed me her heart. What a lovely sense of mission she carried to work every day. I was blessed by her outstanding show of skill and compassion.

My wonderful day nurse was Tracy, who was nearly six feet tall with short blonde hair and a lovely British accent. She was sweet and feisty at the same time, a blend of British and Bostonian stoicism. She was unfailingly attentive, even helping boost my morale by bringing in actual shampoo to replace the hospital stuff and washing my hair every two days. She said my hair was my crowning glory and I shouldn't have to neglect it.

In the midst of administering frequent blood transfusions and IV meds and monitoring Mom's assistance with wound cleaning, she treated me like a person—like *Rebekah* and not just another of her many patients. I don't know if such things can be taught in nursing school. It seemed that Tracy just had this in her nature.

At night the level of care I received was no different. My nurse Naomi, who grew up in Falmouth and is about as Boston as they come, entertained me with her own life stories. She consoled me when my emotions became too much to handle on my own. Whenever she got a few minutes of free time, she would come back to my room to check in on me and oftentimes just sat and watched HGTV to keep me company. She did whatever she could to make me comfortable.

After thirty-two days, the staff decided I could transfer to a rehabilitation center and begin getting ready to go back home. My surgeons told me, "For now you can keep the left leg and try physical therapy; see how it goes." This was a good piece of news. Everyone at the hospital had been so wonderful to me over the past month, but I was hungry to begin putting my life back together.

They transferred me via ambulance to Spalding Rehabilitation Center, where the doctors checked me in and said I looked good, ready to begin transitioning back home after a few more weeks. However, Murphy's Law being what it is, later that day I noticed my left foot turning purple and beginning to swell. Of course, it had looked terrible ever since the blast, but this seemed different. It struck me as dangerous. I called a nurse and pointed it out to her, but at first she didn't notice anything abnormal.

Hours went by, and my foot continued to swell and turn darker in color. I began to really get concerned. The foot pain was growing fierce, even compared to the pain of surgical recovery. And several hours later, when the doctor made his rounds, he took one look and immediately said the foot was infected and they had to send me back to the hospital for treatment.

I made no objection. In spite of all the pain and discomfort of my hospital stay, I had come to trust and rely on the staff in that place. Here, in this new environment, my intuition told me that the more vulnerable my condition was, the more I needed to get back under my hospital's care and not worry about the rehab yet.

Within hours they had me back at the hospital, where immediate exams revealed osteomyelitis, a bone infection, in my more damaged left leg. The next day my doctors grimly informed me that the leg would have to come off. There was no time to watch and wait. The bone infection could quickly spread and prove lethal. They would do an exploratory operation the following day to determine the best place to do the amputation, then perform the main surgery. In the meantime, they kept me loaded with antibiotics to keep the infection from spiraling out of control.

By this point, after so many weeks, I wasn't that surprised to hear this news. My right leg appeared to be recovering and seemed as if it could eventually regain strength. But my left leg had taken much more of the blast, especially the lower leg, simply due to the angle of the explosion. Even after weeks of recovery, it remained barely recognizable to me.

My story takes a sharp turn at this point, something that I can only describe as another miracle. My mother reached out via email, social media, and phone calls to everyone we knew and asked them to pass on her urgent plea for prayer warriors everywhere to pray for me. She heard back from people all over. In answer to her appeal, dozens of people prayed for me that night and the following day. Together they asked God to fill my body with enough strength to battle this new assault on my system.

This was not the first time in life that Mom had asked for prayer for our family—more specifically, for me. And it seemed that each time she did, we were able to comprehend just a little more of how powerful God really is.

The idea of amputation seemed to be for the best, and I hoped that was true, but by that point I had no idea. Events had taken on a heavy, inevitable feel. There wasn't any debate involved over the surgery, or even time to think about it. Before I knew it they were wheeling me down to the surgical bay and putting me under again.

Time jumped, the way it always does with anesthesia— the lights go dark and everything flashes ahead—and the next thing I knew my awareness was returning and I was in recovery.

Pretty soon my doctor came in and explained that when they opened my foot and leg, they discovered that my body had been able to clear the osteomyelitis without the operation. In that very short window of time, an infection that was so bad it threatened my life and made amputation appear necessary had simply . . . gone away.

So they stitched the incision and decided to leave everything in place. "We still want you to keep your leg," he told me, which sounded good, except that this would now involve more hospital time while we watched to be sure the infection didn't reappear, but that was all right with me.

I had never in my life been more thankful for prayer warriors.

One of the ways Mom helped me pass the time and get both our minds off the latest procedure was to maintain my Facebook page for me. There were a lot of posts offering support, and these gave me a tangible feeling of prayers and loving concern. Facebook also let Mom keep our friends and relatives filled in on the news each day. Any positive distraction was welcome.

It was only later that I learned about people posting idiotic conspiracy theories about the Boston bombing being a giant hoax. I realize there are all kinds of viewpoints in the world, and some people still think the world is flat and that Americans never landed on the moon. But I was taken aback when I saw the level of hostility. It, too, was now included in the "new normal." I recognized that I could never go back, in the sense of returning to the old normal, but I would feel unsettled until I could work out what this new normal meant for me and for Noah.

Then there was what I must call a godsend. It began with a wonderful man, a member of our Houston church, who was a stranger to our family until the bombing happened. The congregation had been receiving reports on our recoveries, and he and his wife had heard about Noah and me.

His name was Edd Hendee (I think the second *d* is silent), and he was a local radio host (who retired shortly after the bombing) who did a lot of philanthropic work, partnering with his wife. He had a strong feeling that my recovery would surely go smoother if I could be moved to a hospital closer to home.

Mr. Hendee happened to be in Boston for a ceremony honoring his son, who had passed away years before in a tragic skiing accident. So while he was in town, he called the hospital and arranged to visit with me and my mom. He turned out to be a warm and caring man who was as loving to us as anyone could ask. He put us at ease, insisting that I use his first name. After a bit of general conversation, he told us that he and his wife wanted to personally arrange to get me from Boston back to Houston and into an appropriate hospital there, so I could finish recovering near home, as soon as I was physically able to make the long trip.

I tell you, hearing that offer truly had the effect of parting the clouds, especially coming from this kind stranger who knew of us only because he was a member of our local church. We were so moved by his generosity. There was nothing to do but accept and rejoice at this sudden blessing.

I was eager to go, though I wished I felt more recovered inside. But since I wasn't all that clear on what "recovered" might actually mean, we began getting ready for the move.

Departure day quickly arrived, and it was time for me to be wheeled down to an ambulance to make the ride to the airport. In a moving gesture, the doctors, nurses, and staff lined the hallways and cheered when they rolled me out on my gurney. Naomi came in to say good-bye even though it was her day off.

A small medivac jet was waiting to fly us to Houston. This should have been an exciting moment and a new beginning, but my deep gratitude for this philanthropy didn't protect me from a list of fears and concerns that was growing longer by the minute. I couldn't explain why. I felt a deep restlessness that seemed to radiate from my bones.

Noah and my dad had gone back on a regular commercial flight, but Mom was able to make the trip with me. Even with Mom's support, my anxiety level surprised me by spiking as soon as we left the familiarity of the Boston hospital.

I clenched my teeth and set my jaw against sheer panic while they lifted my gurney from the ambulance, placed it aboard the plane, and strapped it down. The gurney took up most of the room, leaving just enough for Mom, a nurse, and a flight crew of a pilot and copilot. The trip took about two hours. All I could do was be mindful of what we were doing and patiently endure the discomfort of all that movement. In spite of the pain meds I was given for the flight, the trip filled me with dread.

―――

I arrived at Memorial Hermann Hospital in downtown Houston to be greeted by a staff who were clearly determined to treat me with attentive care. While I had no doubts about their professionalism, back in Boston I had formed real bonds with a number of the doctors, nurses, and other staff. We were all comrades in the quest to recover. I didn't realize how much that sense of solidarity had sustained me until it was gone.

At this new hospital, a side effect entered the picture. It didn't take long to present itself and involved all the medicines I'd been taking.

My new doctors were serious about clearing my system of most of the pain drugs before they would consider discharging me to go home. Since I was totally ignorant of the effects of pain med dependency, I confused my subjective condition with an actual need for the drugs. It suddenly felt impossible to bear the physical discomfort and the emotional instability on top of everything else.

The doctors and nurses were politely unsympathetic. This baffled me. Everyone had been so attentive. Suddenly pain was no big deal? I had been blessed to be brought back to my hometown, but it felt as though this had to be a mistake. Why did I hurt this much? And how was I supposed to live with an emotional fragility that wasn't good for anybody?

For me, the PTSD resulting from the whole experience had been pretty well held at bay until now. But suddenly, leaving the womb of the Boston hospital and going out into the world, flying on a small plane, and feeling the torment of increased physical pain all combined to leave me feeling as if I was suffocating. The air felt depleted of oxygen. I was a bony fish out of water.

For nearly five weeks, the repeated assaults of the debriding surgeries had felt like taking a beating every other day from people who like you and who are sorry to have to do it. Even so, up to this point I was spared much of the anxiety and free-floating panic attacks that went on underneath my recovery because I was sedated so often that the chemicals kept them at bay most of the time. I had often felt the suffocating sensations lingering in the back of my mind, but that was all.

Now my return to home territory forced me to consider aspects of the future that I hadn't had to face while I was isolated in a hospital far from home. Noah needed me to get myself back together, even if I still couldn't do a lot of the things I used to do for him, but I had the distinct notion that I was moving backward and everything was falling apart.

Mom quietly endured my rants about "this lousy hospital" and my very helpful suggestions that I needed to go back to Boston, where they "understood" me. Of course, what they understood in Boston, as well as in Houston, was that I had reached the limits of what pain meds could do for me and was entering the realm where the drugs were part of the problem.

At one point I started protesting, "I'm not a drug addict! I legitimately need this medication!"

Thank God my dependency was relatively mild and the doctors were well aware that what I needed was to begin living without so much of the medication. Nevertheless, when I was in the thick of it and tried to imagine a future day when a few aspirin might do the trick, the picture refused to come into focus.

Mom said this was the only time during my entire hospital stay that I failed to be pleasant to the staff. She was sympathetic but she trusted the doctors' judgment on this. To me that felt like some sort of betrayal by my personal advocate.

The professionals in Houston were as skilled and as caring as anyone could ask. They had the difficult job of helping me adjust to being the kid who transfers into a classroom in the middle of the school year, and in that spirit they moved me toward getting ready to go home.

The pain remained. In truth, the pain pulled up a chair right next to me and settled in as part of the new normal.

Although I was still struggling to maintain a prayerful outlook, I did feel myself gain a little strength by having that
as a focal point.

Amid all this, it took a few days before I could see that
the only answer was to cut out the meds.

I'm thankful that my emotional instability went away after
those first few rough days in Houston, once my system was
cleared of most of the heavy chemicals. The artificially dark
tint to my worldview passed. It felt like being barely missed
by a tornado.

# -4-

# Prayer without Words

My mother played a vital role in my recovery, taking care of me and the rest of our family with the same loving dedication she had always shown. It was consistent with the dedication she had shown all of us many years earlier, when she had finally decided that the household was so badly broken that she needed to file a restraining order against my father and move herself and her kids into her parents' home. I was only eight years old.

My grandparents graciously took us in, which allowed Mom to get a full-time job with UPS. We called them Grammy and Grandaddy, and they were both wonderful to us, just as loving as they could be, and my grandaddy was the first close-up experience I can recall of a genuinely loving family man. A true gentleman. I had no idea how blessed I was; I only knew I loved his company.

Until we all left for our new home with our grandparents, the limitations of my youth and inexperience kept me blind to the patience and nobility of my mother's struggle in making this move. When it later became clear to me, it crystalized my concept of what it means to be a Christian woman in today's world.

———

Maybe my sense of helplessness after the bombing would have been just as bad if my background were different. And maybe the torment would have been just as great if helplessness hadn't been a common theme of my early life. But it was, and our pasts shadow us.

My earliest memories are based on an urgent need to recognize the difference between how things look to the outside world and how they actually are, behind closed doors. For people like us, the power of our need to quickly figure out that difference is equal to the danger we face if we fail. Pain is a powerful teacher.

As the eldest of three daughters in the family of a charismatic and handsome preacher, my life appeared idyllic, especially if people didn't get close, which my father managed carefully. But despite appearances, our house was never safe. At home, his charisma dissolved into a petulant and grumbling form of dissatisfaction. It could flare at any given moment and blow up into emotional tirades or truly dangerous rage.

In the days since the bombs went off, I've met too many other people whose background was the same. Even if their circumstances were different on the outside, the reality behind closed doors matched mine. Their home was never safe either.

And so, as a little girl, my primary art and skill became that of avoiding the outbursts. Every time I failed I wound up taking another scorching, with screamed accusations and criticisms over my endless list of flaws. If you've ever showered underneath a flamethrower, you get the idea.

At those moments, that charming man who made the whole family look so good when we were outside the home transformed in my eyes into a dangerous and intimidating creature who prowled our lives in search of a reason to explode. I had learned that the key to dealing with the invisible minefield created by his personality was to rapidly figure out what was genuine and what was false. Doing that helped to minimize the psychological damage inflicted when the blame and accusations were turned toward me.

If we were outside and our smiling father told a neighbor he was taking us inside for ice cream, it was vital to run the past few hours back through my memory in search of anything that might have made him angry. If he was storing up an outburst, then the ice cream story would just be an excuse to get us back inside the house, alone with him.

If I overheard such a thing, I could possibly slip away while he wasn't looking, acting as if I didn't hear him. Then I could manage to avoid being around when it was time to go in.

But since I couldn't get away with running off every time I suspected his motives, the challenge was to figure out the truth and react in an instant. *Stay or go?*

Because the thing is sometimes it would really just be about ice cream or something equally harmless. The dangerous aspect was not knowing which was which. For that reason, I became desperate for authenticity.

And in those times when I couldn't make out the difference between what was true and what was just a dressed-up fake,

I did the only thing I could: I dodged the whole conflict and retreated into a young girl's fantasy life.

That might be the reason my first conscious memories kick in at about age six, which is pretty late into childhood, I must admit. Those memories consist of sitting up in the branches of a backyard tree, removing myself from ground level, where my dangerous home stood. The house itself was nice enough, a parsonage provided by our church. It was the household within it that I couldn't get my head around.

As the eldest sister, maybe it was natural for me to receive so much of the anger. I had more responsibilities, more ways to fail to get the job right, more chances to disappoint.

Some days I walked right through the invisible land mines and it was all fine. On other days, though, one of the many things I did that angered him or one of the little ways I failed to deliver would set off another explosion. No amount of determination in applying myself was enough to keep from causing outrage and being on the receiving end of a harsh and sustained outburst. The physical violence, at that point, was not as big a problem as the scorn and contempt. He kept an internal list to use during his personal tirades, assuring me I would never amount to anything.

Any time he didn't take his anger out on me, he took it out on my mother. And she was his target a lot of other times as well. For years she endured his rages without striking back. She wore her role as the woman of the house like an iron suit, stayed inside it, and tied herself in knots to keep the peace.

For me the long-term effect was rather like the old Chinese tradition of binding a little girl's feet. In our house the bindings were made of my father's rage and contempt. Beneath them, my sense of self became shrunken and deformed.

Those of us who have been through this process know that it happens without producing visible scars, but the effect is no less real.

I was not much older than my son on the day of the bombing when it was made clear to me that I was a major source of turmoil in the home. My father had all sorts of bad news for me in his ongoing list of my failings. It seemed as if the fact that I was in the house at all made him angry.

However, when you are invited to attend your own bashing and are helpless to avoid it, I learned there was nothing else to do but mentally vacate the situation. Head for the trees. We had a big one in the backyard, and I spent a lot of time there.

Today, when there is no longer any threat from him, I can see so easily through an adult's eyes that his anger had little or nothing to do with me and was much more of a reflection of his personal frustration with himself and the circumstances of his life. Of course, back then, when that information may have eased the anxiety of trying to live with him, such knowledge was as hidden from me as any of the universe's great secrets.

———

But when we stepped into the view of others, the head of our family became wonderful. When my father spoke from the pulpit on Sunday mornings, women fell silent in admiring obedience. Men listened and gave knowing nods of agreement. Meanwhile his wife and his daughters sat in the front pew, attentive to his words and bearing witness to his prowess as a family man.

My father's charm gave him power that way. Like a truly great salesman, he made others want to join his team, to agree with him and meet his approval, to ride the wave of good feeling that came from his affable company. He could have sold anything, but his choice was to sell biblical teachings and homilies from the pulpit, pulling a flock around himself like a warm winter blanket. Attendance at his sermons carried the promise of a solid dose of endorphins. He was able to fuel himself on others' hunger for the good feelings his charm provided. You had to love him. You just had to.

If I wasn't careful, I sometimes started to feel rotten for disappointing a man who was so clearly loved and respected by his congregation. What did it mean when such a man held me in contempt? I was too young to unravel his mercurial personality. All I could do was use my hunger for knowledge like a little bloodhound to help in my search for what was true.

Naturally, prayer was a part of my life then. But the experience was hollow. I couldn't connect to the process because prayer itself came from my father's world of church and pulpit. I went through the act of praying, determined to be a good girl, without having a clear idea of what that actually meant. The definition seemed to change with my father's moods.

Eventually, my body took on a deep level of tension that kept me ready to jump away from a blow. That constant fight-or-flight mode did a real number on my ability to be still and know the Lord.

My drive for authenticity and for things that were true, for people or things I could trust, was sparked by all the times I heard his accusations about my failings and somehow understood they were false. To determine what the truth actually was, I had to know exactly what he meant, then compare that to what seemed true to me. If I worked it out, then I could go through the motions of placating him without giving up all of myself and becoming nothing. I would know better.

Some days it worked and some days it didn't.

Back then, I couldn't have told you what was wrong with me, but I had already absorbed the message that I didn't deserve my father's kindness because of my many flaws. My head understood that it wasn't true, but the message seeped in some other way.

For years, my mother was the one who consistently maintained a godly presence in our home, for her husband and all three of us girls. Her role as peacekeeper resulted in her constant litany that when Dad was home, we should just keep quiet and stay out of the way.

So we made this false picture for the world. Back then, I had no idea how many people do their own version of this. So many are stuck in that place at this very moment.

On most Sundays I was able to keep my shortcomings in check and play the role of Obedient Preacher's Daughter. It was the only way to find any peace once we got home. Even at that early stage, I had a major case of OPD.

If you've had to internalize your stresses because it wasn't safe to be honest about them, or if you're in a life situation right now where you can't express yourself with safety, then I'm betting you already know about stress illness. You know from your own experience of it.

And so, even though I had discovered a temporary coping mechanism in the branches of that backyard tree, a little girl's mind tricks couldn't do a thing to protect me once I had to climb down and walk back inside. As anyone who has been in a similar situation knows, the way you get yourself to go back inside a dangerous house—when you have no other choice but to go—is to remember that sometimes your sense of danger will be mistaken. Sometimes your fears will all be for nothing. And maybe *this* time it will be nothing. The Golden Maybe.

So you go. Meanwhile you work on your skills at spotting land mines from a distance.

———

While I was lying on that Boston street, my biological father never once appeared in my thoughts, nor did he do so at any time during that horrible ambulance trip. I didn't play back any images of him during the short time I was still awake in the hospital either. Since Mom had divorced him by the time I was eight, I was accustomed to his absence from both my days and my thoughts.

I know that my mom hated the idea of divorce. It went against everything she felt about the importance of family life. Because of that, she resisted the idea of breaking up the family for years. But she grew so worried by his increasing levels of rage that she finally confided her fears to me: she truly believed he would kill her if she tried to leave. I wonder how many people whisper such things to one another every day, in quiet places and hidden corners. It was awful to hear, but I didn't need convincing. I knew I felt safe only with her and not with him.

In order for Mom to consider leaving my father without leaving her children, she had to walk the tightrope of keeping any plans she might have away from him while also remaining cooperative enough at home to keep a lid on his anger levels. She had to maintain this delicate balance long enough to find a realistic alternative, which meant a full-time job for her and housing for all of us. Beneath the practical nightmare of making such a move there was the emotional torment of any Christian's natural resistance to a cut-and-run approach to marital difficulties. But the equation changed for her when it came to physical safety in the home. She realized both her constancy in that marriage and her patience as a partner were working against her and her children. The situation only degraded our well-being.

And so the breaking point for her turned out to be that same one suffered by mothers in similar situations around the world: the young lives of her children were too vulnerable to risk. She felt we were all in physical danger. The domestic turmoil had to stop.

Amazingly, she survived the separation process without violent conflict, though the divorce was nasty. They split custody of us kids in a sort of 90/10 proportion, with my father taking us on alternate weekends. The understanding was that if he activated his temper, he would lose all access to his children. At the time, some people might have seen my mom's separation as a failure, but others saw it then and will see it now as a brave act by a loving mother on behalf of little girls who could not protect themselves.

Freedom from that oppressive home life was a completely welcome change, as was freedom from a portrayal of a religious life that just never felt authentic to me. Both helped to set me on the path to a much deeper appreciation of what living for Christ means.

They led me to the day I got my first strong tap on the shoulder from Jesus. I was ten years old. Mom and I were on a familiar excursion to the hospital for treatment of yet another asthma attack. I was diagnosed shortly after my parents divorced. These frequently hit me hard enough to require trips to the emergency room while I wheezed and fought to pull air into my lungs on the car ride over.

My mother and I were standing in the hospital elevator. I think we were on our way down to get a chest X-ray. The struggle to breathe tended to make me self-focused, and I was not in a happy state.

It happened there and then.

There was no sense of a divine visitation, though. I never heard a voice. Instead, a bolt of awareness hit me that was too right, too real, and too deep to have come from my young mind. It was caused by a scene that played out right in front of us, when a very small girl was wheeled into our elevator by an attendant.

She was so frail she appeared to be at death's door. I felt a stab of pity. It lasted until she turned to me and hit me with a lovely smile and asked, "Isn't it a beautiful day?"

It wasn't even a question really. It was an affirmation. There was no doubt she meant it. Some form of divine inspiration had replaced this girl's grim ordeal with a revelation of peace and joy that radiated from her. For me, it surpassed all understanding.

I was suffering in my own situation while she found beauty in hers. We only had time to exchange a few words before she left the elevator. I stood watching her go, my own problems forgotten.

Humility was my only possible response. It was a complete revelation to see that girl, so much more ill than I was, finding the beauty surrounding both of us that I had missed. This feeling was new to me. I'd been humiliated at home many times, but an attack on someone's self-esteem doesn't result in humility, only shame.

Those few moments with her made a deep impression on me. She left me wanting to discover the source of her gentle self-assurance. I had made a public profession of faith at age seven and had been baptized by my biological father. But I was far from understanding the Christian faith and from having a living relationship with Christ. My own conflict over what I heard in church and saw in daily life had left me alternating between faith and fear.

True prayer entered my life for the first time on that day. This was not prayer as an imitation of the behavior expected from an Obedient Preacher's Daughter but rather prayer that was an act of reaching out from the deepest parts of myself to commune with a loving God.

Of course, my spiritual eyes were just beginning to open, and while I had been led through all the motions of baptism and biblical teachings, I was not yet saved in the sense of fully and consciously embracing Christ. That was yet to come.

Still, my journey began back there in that elevator. It was ignited by grace delivered by a beatific child whose load was heavier than my own. That frail little girl showed me the direction of the Lord's footsteps. She didn't have to speak a challenge for me to follow her; she embodied the challenge.

More than anything else, that's what she awakened in me: a true sense of having a direction to follow, as opposed to simply knowing what I was expected to say and do.

I was still a long way from living my life in Christ and had to overcome my background of what I saw as religious falsehood and spiritual emptiness. But now I was hungry to know peace within.

It was not a booming revelation; it was more like the first thin ray of sunrise. The peaceful silence of my old perch up in the backyard tree was replaced by a drive to live somehow closer to the Holy Spirit. I had no idea how to proceed, since all the skills my background provided seemed phony and ineffective. My steps would be small and slow, but for the first time I could sense the direction I needed to travel.

———

When the bombs went off in Boston and while I was still fighting an uncertain battle in the hospital, my sense of responsibility for my son filled me with the will to rejoin life with him. Today I realize I got the model for this kind of determination from my mother. That goal seemed impossibly high for a while, and when I dared to think ahead and imagine how we might actually get along in the world, I couldn't envision a way out. But what I missed at the time was that my prayers were already being answered. My drive to make that life with Noah happen helped to keep me strong.

This was again mirroring my mother's way of living in Christ. She was never one to preach the gospel in my face or to wave a sense of righteous superiority around.

She never had to harp on the lesson that talk is cheap and that what you *do* is who you really are. She just lived it out every day and made it real. Faith may be invisible, but its effect on behavior is not. She taught by doing, and it's hard to argue with what you see before your eyes. I didn't have much to rebel against.

As a girl, I straddled the clear reality of my mother's faith and spiritual dedication on the one side and the distorted notion of Christianity I had learned as an Obedient Preacher's Daughter on the other. The result was that my conscious spiritual life nearly shut down altogether while the part of me that learned by example continued to absorb the message that there had to be something more, something greater than me.

Every eight-year-old girl wants to idolize her mom. My loyalty to Mom and to what I felt to be the truth caused me to admire her and want to be more like her. At the same time, my father's whole world represented treachery to me. I'm certain he saw it differently, but that's the effect it had on me. My sophistication was inadequate to tease apart those influences and pull the truth away from the falsehoods.

This battle within me wasn't going to resolve itself overnight. And by the time Mom pulled us out of there, I had already developed a coping mechanism I call the Sad Skill. I gave it that name because a skill takes real effort to learn, and the more this skill is used the more harm it does to the user. It is a skill of avoidance, temporarily delivering peace—or at least the absence of conflict—but pushing honesty under the carpet.

A person with the Sad Skill has the ability to thoroughly stuff negative thoughts and emotions deep, way down deep, maintaining instead a relentlessly cheerful demeanor and an inoffensive conversational style. When we employ the Sad Skill, it comes to be our expected mode. People tend to like it because we are giving away our energy and taking little in return. The bars that trap us inside the Sad Skill are made of other people's expectations, but they're created by our own behavior.

I only realized years later that the Sad Skill is widely employed, found in every walk of life. Furthermore, in the days since the Boston Marathon bombing, I've learned from the testimony of others that the unseen prison of the Sad Skill only grows in strength over time. It did with me, and I resonate with the stories people shared with me.

As a young girl, I got through my days by shutting down my feelings and personal needs in favor of pleasing anyone else who happened to be around. For me, the concept of feeling good seemed vaguely obscene. I wasn't good enough to feel good. Indelible memories of my father's tirades rebounded in the form of a compulsive drive to look good, smile big, and make others happy.

This is the Sad Skill at its heart. It's not about bravely soldiering on in the face of things that can't be changed, as almost anyone has to do from time to time and as some people do throughout their lives. It's about hiding your pain so well that you even conceal it from yourself, assuring that everyone stays as content as possible while nothing gets fixed.

My self-appointed role became the "guardian of tempers," seeing to it that nobody ever had a reason to be upset about anything. Or if somebody did happen to become angry or even mildly irritated, my self-declared responsibility was to make them feel better as quickly as possible, whether I had done anything to cause the problem or not.

I'm sure you already recognize this as a self-destructive choice. I do now—I didn't then. With all the logic of one who has wandered away from God, I responded to my hunger by refusing to eat, falling back into old negative patterns that were more deeply ingrained than I realized. This made faith hard in those days, and today I believe similar forms of emotional trauma make it hard for many others.

Too often, when I prayed, it was only to fulfill the obligation to speak certain words into the air. That way if anyone was watching, I'd make a convincing "good girl" show and there wouldn't be any trouble.

*Part Two*

# FINDING
# *My* WAY

# -5-

# The Visitation Blues

My father's visitation rights involved us girls spending every other weekend with him. His congregations knew him as their pastor. Of course, we saw the extent of his flaws, which must be true for anyone who lives with a preacher. As the oldest child, I'm sure the impression was strongest with me.

Any spiritual progress I made in those years happened of its own accord, outside the church and religion. It was powered by the enduring hunger left over from those brief moments, such as the moment in the elevator, when I felt what I can only describe as the presence of God.

By then I was old enough to understand that Mom had no choice in the visitation arrangement. If she challenged it in court and things went badly because he could outspend her on lawyers, or if his attorney worked up some unexpected legal move, she could be forced to give us over to him. I found the idea unthinkable, and so I was happy enough with everything about the visitation arrangement except the visitation.

As a newly single mother, my mom became the unstoppable worker bee. Once she got a good job and put away some money, we moved from her parents' home to our own place while she kept plugging along, working and parenting on her own. During the next few years, my old demon of helplessness hit hard again while I watched her endure conditions so much harsher than she deserved.

She honored the custody agreement and surrendered all three of us to him on those alternate weekends. I knew, from the way she was with us the rest of the time, that she would have gladly filled her resulting private time with our company if she could have. That same measurement was the reason I was so uncomfortable in my father's new reality as an itinerant preacher, one who was sometimes attached to one church, sometimes operating freelance, and skilled enough at dealing cards to always have paying casino work when God failed to provide. He wasn't there much, even when we were at his place.

I know there was a part of him that wanted to be a good dad, or at least I like to think there was such a part of him. On visitation weekends, he may have been having such a difficult time of it on the personal level that he just couldn't manage the energy needed to take care of us. I do remember one happy occasion when he sat us down to learn blackjack. It seemed like a harmless game, something we could all do together. We were happy because he used cookies for chips.

I always saw him as having terrible financial problems, and there was often very little to eat in his kitchen. He also had to work on many occasions when we were with him, so I wound up taking care of my sisters. The sense of responsibility was heavy because there was little I could do for them and not much comfort for us in that place. There were times when my own anger and resentment felt poisonous to me. Of course, the Obedient Preacher's Daughter walled off most of those feelings.

This went on for several years after the divorce, until one day Mom sat me down with my sisters and told us she had been dating a man for a while and that they really liked each other a lot. She said his name was Tim Gregory, and it was time for us to meet him.

Within the following year, they were married. Tim proved himself to be an honorable man who was up to the challenge: taking on marriage, his first, to a woman with three young girls. I was thirteen at the time, and during my fourteenth year, Tim officially adopted me and my sisters.

Sounds sweet, doesn't it? Almost greeting card-ish? It actually was, once all the dust settled. It's just that the dust filled the air for a long time. A good share of that was my fault. Because I was so out of touch with my feelings, in my commitment to my role as an OPD, I had no idea how much suspicion I held toward any male who might have some sort of authority over me. When a new man was added to that mix—one with access to my mother—I saw nothing but trouble.

The poor guy had his work cut out for him. And it's not like Tim is a creampuff. He wasn't about to try to beg his way into our hearts, and if he softened his tendency toward sarcastic humor when we were around, I sure couldn't tell. A few times one of us would try to "refuse" to go someplace when Mom attempted to take us somewhere with her and Tim, but they weren't having a lot of that nonsense.

What we experienced with Tim was the opposite of what I experienced with my father. My father had seemed as though he really didn't want to spend time with us and that we weren't worth the effort. Tim wasn't going to beg us to love him, but contrary to all expectations, he wasn't going to go away either.

As time went on and his relationship with my mom continued to bloom, more than anything else, all three of us girls couldn't avoid noticing that Tim was always there for us. He always showed up for the family, and he seemed to think we were important enough for his valuable time. He also treated us all with loving respect. Even at that age, I had a pretty good idea that this was a wonderful thing. And so keeping up an angry wall against Tim started to feel like a lot of work. I began to wonder what my objections were supposed to be.

In terms of my desire for a healthy and permanent family, in some ways it pains me to admit that I would have gladly lived with Mom and Tim on a full-time basis from the beginning. It wasn't that I had no affection for my father, but in my eyes he was dangerously unpredictable. His emotional explosions were so frightening that I was completely unable to appreciate the other ways in which he may have fulfilled his role as our father. It felt like trying to accept being kissed on the cheek when it might be followed by a blow, or walking on the floor of a house with unseen places where you would fall through if you stepped there, but you never knew where they were.

After the separation, it was wonderful to have peace in the house at last, to come home and open the door without anxiety. But there is heavy emotional weight behind the idea that your home is a broken place. For the next three years, the thought of coming from a broken home was fresh in my mind. It had to be, because it was kept fresh in the minds of my peers by the visitation blues.

My sisters and I arrived at school on visitation Fridays carrying little suitcases packed for the weekend. We could stash these in the administration office for the day, but on Friday afternoons, when all the kids and their parents were streaming by, we had to sit on our suitcases and wait for my father to pick us up. Sometimes he showed up and sometimes he didn't.

I know everyone has their story, and I'm sure he could explain how it happened, but on our end of things we were just out there, curbside. If he didn't show, we had to go back into the office and have someone call Mom, who would have to leave work to come and get us. We all know how much bosses love it when their employees have to suddenly leave work because of their kids.

Let's see, now: Did any of the other kids notice my sisters and me out there with our suitcases? Ahem. It might have been more obvious if we had sat under a Hollywood-sized spotlight, but there was plenty of attention to go around. Somebody started the rumor that our father was a "jailbird" and that this was why we lived with him only on weekends.

Of course, the rumor stuck. Kids would catcall while we sat on our suitcases, "Where's your jailbird father?" A few of them openly predicted that the reason he didn't show must be that he was "in jail again, ha, ha!" Good times.

I don't know if I consciously withdrew from my classmates or if they just moved away from me, but those suitcases brought a lot of alone time into our school experience for my sisters and me. Whether or not my sisters understood the terms the older kids used, I know they felt the sting of ridicule clearly enough.

Visitation meant a weekend with my father's unpredictable moods and with what I considered to be his distinct personalities. On a good day, we got the happy preacher teaching us card games. More often than not, though, we got the angry and offended man I knew too well. As the oldest, I carried the most responsibilities, but I was apparently a constant disappointment. Leaving a toy out, forgetting to make a bed, or getting caught watching an unapproved TV show could invoke outbursts of rage. I could tell that these responses were much too ferocious for the incident, but there wasn't much I could do to shield my younger sisters from his rants. As the oldest, a lot of it came my direction anyway.

The visitation blues played its last stanza while we were at our father's house for one particular weekend. It was a small place in a bad neighborhood, and he was gone for the day. It was hot outside, a real scorcher, and the air-conditioning window unit wasn't working. For a while, we tried to pass the time by playing outside, but not only was it sweltering we also didn't feel comfortable outdoors without an adult in that neighborhood. At least there was shade inside. So we went in where we felt safer, but in spite of the wide-open windows there wasn't enough breeze to keep the room comfortable at all.

My sisters and I got along well enough, but they had no idea why we had to sit around in heated misery instead of just being back at home with Mom. At least they always brought toys from home to keep themselves busy, so we all just sat around in the stifling heat marking time. It could have been worse; at that point our father was dating frequently and oftentimes brought his dates home. On this day we were glad to be there by ourselves without having to also deal with our father and some other woman.

The afternoon wore on. Time dragged. The temperature inside got so hot that the house felt like a cross between a steam room and a sauna. My sisters began to get really distressed, so I took them into the bathroom and put us all in the shower, under the cool water. That was my best idea, and although I was only eleven at the time, even today I don't know what else we could have tried. It worked well enough for a while, but it was quickly obvious that we couldn't spend the day in a shower. None of us were at all clear on why we were having to go through all this. My sisters felt trapped and stranded, and I didn't know what to tell them.

Their distress finally made me break down and call my mom, which was a real blow to my pride. Even though I was terrified of the punishment I could receive from our father for doing that, I was serious about my responsibilities as the older sister. I knew there was no one else to take care of them at that house and the situation on that day left me with no other tools.

So I explained to my mom that we were stuck in the stifling house by ourselves and had been alone for hours, and I was out of ideas on how to keep my sisters calm. I told her we didn't understand why we had to be present for "visitation" when our father wasn't there to do any visiting.

She stopped what she was doing and called the police, who came to get us, and Mom met us down at the station. We were out of there before he came home. It was our last visit.

The next day she got a restraining order against him and then took him to court. My dad wound up signing over his rights to all three of us, and that, at last, was the end of the visitation blues.

He let go. We moved on. I never looked back.

By that time, we girls had spent enough time with Mom and Tim not only to warm up to Tim's presence but also to be acutely aware of the difference in how he treated her, as opposed to how we saw our father treat her. Nobody needed to lecture us about it.

How refreshing it was to come home and be happy to walk in the door without that cringing feeling that braces you for trouble. We now knew firsthand how it felt to have peace in the house.

Peace in the house. It's comfort for the soul. Test everything else that goes on in your home against the idea of peace in the house. Anything that passes this test is good for you. We had waited a long time for this.

About a year after Mom and Tim got married, when he formally adopted all three of us, we started calling him Dad. He had never been married before Mom came along with us three girls. I honor the courage of any man who would do such a thing. Although I'm afraid we made him work for his welcome, not only did he do exactly that but the process also gave him plenty of time to get to know us and see what he was getting himself into. He embraced the whole thing.

After the visitation ended and our home life stabilized, this new peace in the house was like water in the desert, but it didn't undo the counterfeit "lessons" my childhood mind took from everything leading up to the divorce. Any child who survives a dangerous home will go on and perhaps do well in life or even achieve great things. But every instance of unearned anger or unacceptable insult lands hard, like a heavy stone, and the memory of it remains.

The poisonous lessons I took from the broken marriage had to do with never again allowing myself to be responsible for a disappointed father—or for being a disappointment at all. I vowed to make sure everyone around me was happy and became a dedicated people pleaser, turning up the Sad Skill to maximum power.

No pressure.

We children of divorce, as adults, can easily look back and see how wrong we were during those years to assume there was anything we could have done to keep the family together. But at the time I had no tools for measuring any of those things. I had to let that part go.

The way out was to keep it light. Keep it all smiles around friends within our church congregation as well as friends from school. The Sad Skill helped me to avoid conflict but it also isolated me in a shell of well-intended falsehood.

I've met many people, Christian and nonChristian, who've described the dangers of getting lost in the attempt to please others to one's own detriment. Like them, I successfully managed to avoid setting off family outbursts at home but I failed to realize that there weren't going to be outbursts like that in our new home. And in our old home I hadn't been the one causing them, not even when I was the focal point of the reverend's rage.

When you're dysfunctional you remain blind to simple logic and ignore evidence that is right in front of your face. And so I never felt safe in letting my guard down. This was not a reaction to our new household with Tim; it was a measure of how sticky those explosive episodes from our prior household remained for me.

I made weak attempts to discuss this with my mom but at age fourteen I couldn't articulate the problem. With a level of naïvety that I hope I've now left behind with my girlhood, I entered a period of spiritual hollowness without even realizing it.

---

My father's itinerant preaching moved him from one church to another, and he alternated his pulpit work with the night shift at a local casino. I'm sure he could explain that combination, but for me it added to my already suspicious view of his version of religion.

On the one hand, there were rare occasions when I could feel the hint of God's presence in my life, just enough to keep my heart open to him. But on the other hand, the religious demands, rules, and expectations, as I heard them from my father, felt more like things a lawyer would say in a court of law—harsh and full of condemnation, delivered with angry rants. I could feel my heart burning up. I felt my life with my father to be nothing like a life following Christ and that it contained nothing at all that brought to mind a loving God. But I was still too young to separate the message from the messenger.

I avoided turning to Scripture for guidance because I had heard Scripture used so often to justify outbursts. The rage and violence of those outbursts were presented as righteous anger and legitimate punishment, but they were at a level far beyond anything that today, as a parent myself, I could ever call legitimate.

I could clearly remember childhood moments of feeling close to the Lord and also feeling certain I would never lose touch with his presence. Especially when I was up in that backyard tree. But those lovely moments had become memories of things I no longer repeated.

I was in the proverbial closet—the Obedient Preacher's Daughter, pretending to be a Christian while I went through church rituals that felt unnatural. I couldn't have told you what I did or didn't believe about God with any certainty.

In the days since the Boston Marathon bombing, it's been remarkable to have met so many people whose past experiences match mine, in terms of how their spiritual wakefulness was boosted not just by their relationship with the Lord but also by their relationship to their place of worship. But for some the opposite was true, and they were damaged by the personalities they found there. That was also the case for me.

At the time there was no way for me to tell if I could ever find a personal, deep relationship with God. I suppose the hollow smile of a "church lady" begins with the hollow smile of an Obedient Preacher's Daughter.

# -6-

# All Hat, No Cattle

I spent my teen years as a chameleon, seeking out a variety of crowds and becoming whatever was needed in order to fit in. Most of the time I was too good for my own good. If I couldn't be bouncy and cheerful, I could at least keep quiet about any turmoil of my own. And I did so as if I were on a mission, though I had no idea what that mission was supposed to be.

Even if the exterior of your story is vastly different from mine, you may resonate with the challenge of being spiritually alive and socially acceptable at the same time. I was that way too, but while the desire to fit in is a common concern, I took it to the nth degree.

It felt normal to do that, which means it looked pleasant to others. The Sad Skill schooled me on how easy it is to become your own worst enemy beneath a layer of falsehood, no matter how well intended it may be.

If I had been more honest with myself then, I might have done something to open up and relieve the unnecessary pressure of a hidden existence. But I spent the next four years letting the motions of going to church and singing hymns and praying out loud substitute for a living spiritual life. Combining that with my self-appointed role as a people pleaser on steroids, I trapped my emotions behind locked doors, and they reacted by building up to the point that I became a human pressure cooker. Ironic, I know, but true.

Since I was still a relatively timid sixteen years of age, I certainly wasn't the type to explode and take it out on others, but all that energy had to go somewhere. So it blew through my immune system instead and shorted out my physical health.

A sudden onset of dizziness and fainting spells hit me and refused to go away. These fainting spells became frequent and dangerous. It got to the point that if I had been sitting or lying down for any period of time, a wave of dizziness would hit me when I stood up. It was sometimes so strong I had to sit back down and get up again very slowly. Sometimes I became lightheaded for no discernible reason and would stumble or fall down. Naturally, this was hard on anyone I was with, only in a different way; they were left with the task of explaining to themselves what they were seeing.

Jokes about being tipsy got old fast.

I was too blind to the cause and effect to deal with the core problem. However, the medical explanation emerged when my doctor diagnosed Postural Orthostatic Tachycardia Syndrome (it helps if you read it out loud). Thankfully, it's also abbreviated with the acronym POTS. This neurological illness involves the brain sending out the wrong signals when it comes to adjusting heart rate and blood pressure. It has a severe impact on normal movement. The illness is more serious with adults, since it can stay with them for life. Fortunately for me, it only has an average course of two to five years when it strikes teenagers and young adults. After that, this illness, which is not well understood, runs out of steam for reasons that are also not well understood but that are fine with me.

POTS tends to strike people who have suffered physical trauma or teenagers whose bodies undergo great stressors. Sound familiar? The warning lights were blinking away, bells were ringing, and buzzers were going off.

If I had been in a more spiritually awake condition, I believe my resilience could have been strengthened by my struggles. Instead, the conflict I carried around inflicted such damage on my physical system that it left me with potentially deadly fainting spells.

As you would expect, my ill health affected everything I did. On bad days it was a problem to leave the house at all. It seems clear to me today that this illness spanned the border between mind and body. I look back on it as a manifestation of my self-styled emotional prison. These short circuits in the brain's signals were the result of living inside a pressure cooker of my own making, boiling over heat I put there myself. There seemed to be no end to the cost of living as an Obedient Preacher's Daughter.

For the next four years, the illness remained stronger than I was, until I reached the age of twenty. That's when it slowly tapered off. I had no sense of control over any of it. To me the whole thing felt as if it had showed up without warning, operated on its own schedule, and departed when it was done.

For this, my faltering faith just couldn't rise to the occasion. Even though I became aware, for the first time, of what you could call "the bigness beneath every small thing," and I believe Jesus was reaching out to me, his whispers were lost on me. I was clenched too tightly to respond. Regular trips to the hospital were a part of my life. It felt as if my father's words, the ones stuck in my memory, were prophecy: I was weak and I really would turn out to be good for nothing.

My downhill slide was powered by my own confusion. On the surface I was not a rebellious kid and I appeared to be in sync with my peers. I mostly did whatever I was told by someone in authority.

But that was all exterior work. My inner life, prayer life, and determination to live in Christ were starving. A Texan phrase applies: I was all hat and no cattle.

Under the persistent drip of POTS symptoms, I could never tell when my neural wiring would betray me. The social isolation I had already experienced was amplified now, and each new blood pressure episode landed on the fertile soil of that old voice echoing up from my memory, assuring me that my body certainly couldn't be trusted, since I myself could not be trusted to do anything right.

I became extremely shy in public but remained outgoing at home, almost like two different people. Back then I had no idea how many shy people are like that. I was already a reader, so I became a reader big-time. I could lose myself in books and further developed a love for expressive writing and storytelling.

But as far as my self-worth was concerned, the takeaway was that I was worthless and bound to remain that way. I wasn't conscious of having that viewpoint; it just felt true. I befriended everybody but myself.

For those years, the Obedient Preacher's Daughter was my fallback position. When I was able to go to school and attend outside functions, I could make myself seem to fit in, but I seldom let anyone get close. My father was long gone, but the messages from my childhood held me firmly in their grasp.

# -7-

# Dangle Time

In the weeks after the Boston Marathon bombing, I could feel the same temptation to despair that was such a problem during my teens. The feeling had a heavy downward pull to it, like swimming with a weight belt.

The difference, this time, came in moments of clarity that I didn't have back then. Those moments, brief as they were, were like dappled bursts of light amid the grim tapestry of the hospital routines. They bolstered my heart in the midst of the constant physical assaults from the drumbeat of surgeries every second or third day.

Such moments allowed me to perceive the unique ways that my injuries set me apart from my prior self. Each of them was a reminder of what the Sidewalk Prophets were talking about when they sang "if I need to be still give me peace for the moment." As everyone who suffers traumatic injury knows, our limitations will confront us throughout our recoveries, all day, every day, and it was no different for me.

I developed an ongoing process, matching up the differences between that old normal and this new one in the back of my mind. This all went toward learning how to be this new version of myself.

It was an urgent effort. As soon as I settled in at the Houston hospital and got my head clearer for the transition back home, it was time for a more invasive surgery than any of the operations I had gone through in Boston. We were still fighting to save my left leg, so my surgeon removed a large flap of my back muscle and surrounding tissue to fill the hole in my left foot, where the chunks of bones and surrounding muscle had been blown away. The intention was to give new flesh something to build on.

They also peeled another large rectangle of skin from my outer thigh to cover the foot graft. This thigh wound had to be kept moist for many days after the operation, regularly cleaned, and then re-covered by artificial new skin to keep the infection that was already there from the remaining shrapnel at bay.

The graft on my left foot required the entire leg to be elevated at all times at a level above my heart. In the first two weeks, I couldn't lower it even for a moment or else the shift in blood pressure to the newly forming vessels would likely burst them. No doubt we can all visualize the technical challenges involved in constantly keeping one leg elevated above your heart for twenty-four hours a day without needing to hear further details.

Once that critical two-week period passed without problems, the doctors deemed me ready to go home. I still had to keep my leg elevated, but now I could have five minutes a day of what they referred to as Dangle Time.

Five minutes of Dangle Time might not sound like a big deal. Oh, but it was. It still is, every time I think of it. Consider the joy of a young dog released into a big, sunny yard after a night spent in a cold basement. That's Dangle Time.

Within those brief few minutes, I could hang my legs over the side of the bed and even use the bathroom. True, I still couldn't take a shower instead of using the tub, and I couldn't piddle around in there (five minutes passes quickly). But Dangle Time was a chance to come up for air and remind myself that the whole idea was to get back to independent movement.

Mmm, Dangle Time. It would almost (operative word, *almost*) be worth it to go through elevating your leg over your heart for two weeks just to feel the exquisite relief of simply being able to lower it back to a normal position. Let's return for a moment to that excited young canine bounding out of the basement and into a sunny yard. A world of possibilities.

We learn to be grateful for crumbs. And the experience of gleeful freedom is hardly limited to dogs, since those few minutes a day no doubt feel the same way to a locked-down convict. Five minutes in the exercise yard, kiddo. Spend 'em wisely. Anytime is good time if it's Dangle Time. And so even though Dangle Time for me only meant a few minutes in a vertical position, still: Hallelujah!

---

After those seventeen days in Houston's Memorial Hermann Hospital, it was time to try going home. The doctors and staff there had been kind and professional during my stay, and I alternated every few minutes between being eager to be gone and afraid to make the jump. I yearned to resume a home life with Noah, but I still felt so weak. There were weeks and months of in-home nursing care and recuperation ahead.

Every new day seemed to be a bigger battle than the day before. I was mentally and physically exhausted. But once the schedule was in place, I committed to going through with it. On June 10, fifty-six days after the Boston Marathon attacks, they wheeled me down to my mom's van and propped my leg on pillows for the ride home, ready or not.

Somebody slid the van door closed, and we were on our way. For the time being, Noah and I were going to be at my parents' house, because I needed so much bedside care. I had already been on IV antibiotics in the hospital and had to continue with the IV for six more weeks at home. A health nurse had to come every day to change the dressings on my wounds.

My left foot looked like something that belonged on an alien creature, a misshapen appendage with purple-yellow coloring. The graft had to be checked throughout the day to watch for possible tissue rejection. To keep it from failing, a Heparin shot was to be administered into my stomach every night to prevent blood clots.

It's more accurate to say it would be injected at night into what was left of my stomach. At my final hospital weigh-in, I tipped the scales at seventy-nine pounds. This is just a bit more than half of my healthy body weight. The long slog of surgeries, anesthesia, and appetite-killing opioids had turned me into a convincing portrait of a patient sent home to die.

My fantasy of going home and returning to a life that I still recognized was pretty badly shaken by the reality of the experience. Somehow, in preparing to transition out of the hospital and into home recovery, I visualized myself as being closer to normal health, as if returning to my home environment would somehow restore the old normal that it represented.

Not that I thought I'd be cartwheeling around the front yard, but my images of home life in recent years were happy ones, and I was strong in all of those scenes. The abrupt surprise was in returning to those places only to get another jolt from the new normal.

Unlike the healthy and independent woman I had been, in this new normal I still had the same ongoing needs that had been addressed in the hospital. Only now they had to be taken care of at home, by family members. Our backup was to dial 911 if the wounds became septic, and that was it.

My brief experience at the Spaulding Center had taught me how quickly our bodies can fall to infection, so I had a healthy respect for watching over the surgical and shrapnel wounds. This meant that the road ahead would require a lot of energy from the rest of my family.

That didn't change the fact that after years of being on my own, it was hard on my ego to intrude on my parents' home this way. My youngest sister, Allie, was only eleven at the time, and the sudden change in her home life was far from ideal. It had to be hard on her, but she pitched in and helped me with the challenge of washing my hair with my leg elevated, among other things.

How blessed I was to have this support system and such loving people around me. Consider any victim of a massive injury who must return home to live alone or recover in the hands of strangers. No doubt their degree of difficulty is amplified many times over. I would have had to remain institutionalized or have constant in-home care for many weeks to come if not for all these people and their loving concern.

I've saved the best for last in this chapter because it really is the secret of how I was able to face this phase of the recovery with a brave heart. I say that even though I was fighting off a full-blown panic attack by the time Mom's van pulled up to the house and it was time to wheel me in.

In that panicked state, I was suddenly overwhelmed by the tasks ahead. The ride home from the hospital made me fearful of yet another inexplicable attack from a random source of evil. By the time we pulled up to the house I had convinced myself there was dire danger in every direction. It was that same sudden sense of doom that anyone who has experienced a panic attack would recognize. Real or imaginary, the sense of danger tightened around my neck like a noose and left me gasping for air.

When the van door opened and Mom and Dad prepared to lift me out, Noah came running up, full of infectious delight to have his mom home again. And it was then, with one sentence, that my little boy turned my panic into determination.

"Don't worry, Mom," Noah whispered into my ear while he leaned over to hug me. "We're never leaving this house again."

He said it to console me, of course, to let me know the worst was over. But he unintentionally made his own trauma clear and, in that instant, slapped my panic attack right back out of me.

I couldn't allow myself to be fearful or to withdraw from the world because my son had to be able to go out and engage with that world. There was no way I could allow him to think he should hide from life, even though he had encountered terrorism and its evil work so early in his own. His recovery was tied to mine.

And so, just as he had done for me at the finish line of the marathon, when my concern for him kept me rooted to the spot and determined to see to his survival, he focused my aim once again, simply by virtue of his presence in my life and his love for me, reminding me that being his mom was the central blessing of my time in this world.

The dreaded new normal became a bit less frightening after that. The old normal was gone, but I was home.

*Part Three*

# HIDING *from* SHADOWS

## -8-

# Pushing the River

I was twenty when Noah was born. When I became pregnant at the age of nineteen, my relationship with Christ was strictly formal, all too hollow at the core. I was absent without leave, and the consequences spun my life's path off at a sharp angle.

I was still in college and working to help pay bills, and I wasn't centered enough to realize that my way of making myself "safe" was unhealthy, with all this weird social conformity I felt compelled to use. All sorts of sharp costs began to hit me as a result of surrendering my own will to others.

After graduating high school, I had gone to Eastern Kentucky University intending to study nursing. But after a year of that, my sister Lydia became ill with heart trouble. I moved back home to Lagrange, Kentucky, to get a job and be closer to my family.

I wandered onto the wrong pathways.

I started hanging out again with a guy I'd known in high school when we both worked part-time jobs in the same town. At that time, we had been only friends. Now that I was back home from college, we were both at a New Year's Eve party I hosted at my new apartment—the birthday of a mutual friend of ours happened to fall on the same day, and there was a lot of drinking.

He stayed that night when I should have sent him home. This behavior was so uncharacteristic for me that by morning I felt steeped in guilt and was filled with a sense of lingering dread. Talk about an emotional hangover. I was about to get smacked with the brutal reality of how fast things can happen if we lower our spiritual guard, even for a short time.

Two weeks later, a home test confirmed that I was pregnant. The impact of this news was like the floor giving way and dropping me into a pit. I have to confess that under these circumstances, the miracle of birth and the joy of parenting were not my first thoughts. The crush of responsibility was like a ton of rock, with my self-respect buried somewhere beneath it.

Since we can't make up for a mistake by making another, I was faced with the realization that there was no way to keep this from my parents. And no way to sugarcoat the news. It could hardly be concealed for any length of time. If I waited that long, it would surely be seen as a betrayal.

So I had to go and admit my foolishness to two people I greatly admired, whose good opinion of me was most essential at that time in my life. In order to simply wake up and start moving around in the day and feel okay about myself, I needed their good esteem.

My true spiritual bottom-out occurred days later, on the drive over to my parents' house to let them know. They were, and are, devout people. I knew their Christianity was sincere and that they lived their lives with a strong sense of the importance of honorable behavior. And now I had to bring them this news of my personal lapse in judgment and of the unplanned results. My heart felt like it sat about six inches too low.

I'm grateful to say that for all of their disappointment and pain—which were abundant—their love didn't fail me. There was never any talk of aborting my child. Any regrets they might have had about the manner of conception were tempered by the knowledge that a new member of the family was now on the way. The rest of our concerns had to be about bringing a healthy child into the world.

Their kindness prompted me to do everything I could to own all of the consequences of my choices and to protect this new child. I would work as many hours as possible to prepare for taking care of this baby and find ways to continue my education once my child was born to maximize our chances of having what we needed.

I welcomed the child in spite of my concerns over my failure of judgment. I knew what it was to have a deeply loving and dedicated mother, and I was filled with the desire to let that boy or girl know what it was like to be brought up in the world by a loving mother who could be trusted. I wanted to honor the gift of life by bringing a healthy baby to term and then nurturing him or her with all of my love and energy.

So while I realized that my sense of guilt brought nothing to the table, my loss of self-confidence was a real obstacle when it came to visualizing answers and solutions. I didn't lose my faith in the Lord, but faith in my own judgment collapsed.

In that state of mind, I began the pregnancy determined to fix everything with a relentlessly positive attitude. My sense of shame overcame my faith in redemption, and I covered it all with smiles. I also went from being determined to being obsessive, at work and at home, as if a single mistake would break it all. I wouldn't allow myself to put real trust in God's plan for me. I remained a closed loop while I pushed myself to work harder.

As a result, before long my physical resistance was shot. Apparently, I have one of those bodies that works as a spiritual circuit breaker. Five months into the pregnancy I went into preterm labor and was admitted into the hospital, where I was told that I would stay until it was safe to have the baby.

The doctor's plan worked, and after uncomfortable bed rest and around-the-clock monitoring, three months later a healthy baby boy was born. Suddenly, my new son, my little boy Noah, was there with us all. It was time for Mommy to deal with life as a duo.

I know I was experiencing a deepened relationship with God just because of Noah and the miracle he turned out to be. I was thankful beyond words for the blessing of this child, but I thought this meant I owed some kind of spiritual loan, meaning that I didn't deserve the grace that was there for me.

I forgot that grace isn't something you earn. It is given freely.

Naturally, I never thought of it that way then. Why is that so hard to see in the moment? Because I missed it. I just squinted harder and leaned into the wind.

# -9-

# The Mom Machine

I became a mom machine after Noah was born, focusing on getting every moment right. I had wonderful parents who were willing and able to help me care for him, which meant I could go to work and know he was safe.

I had taken a job at a dialysis clinic, where they trained me to be a dialysis technician. It was a short drive to the clinic but a large cultural leap. That part of town had taken a drastic downturn and was now a seamy neighborhood that seemed to ooze hard-luck stories. I worked twelve- to fifteen-hour shifts, three days a week, and reported for work at four in the morning. It took us two hours to prepare the chemical mixtures used in the filters, see to it that all the machines got set up, and get the clinic ready to receive patients when the doors opened at six. I was often there until six or seven in the evening.

A few of the patients were children or adults with inherited kidney problems, but many of the patients had physical systems weakened by alcohol or drugs, and the fact that they had life stories to match was often plain on their faces. Although I was hardly a sheltered child, some of those individuals showed levels of misery and desperation so extreme that they cried out to me.

It was a constant study in human nature to witness the way that enduring difficulties will cause some people to shrivel into bitterness while others will find their strength and rise to the occasion. I didn't know it then, but I was in the middle of a lesson in empathy. Many of the patients became quite familiar to me, and I felt attached to them. Their welfare, as far as this vital process was concerned, felt personally important to me beyond the call of the job.

You see where I'm going with this, right? How could I have known that I was being shown the stuff I would need to survive down the road? Does God help prepare us in advance for traumatic events, or was this truly a happy coincidence?

No matter where you come down on that, in the stories of these men and women who appeared to be so different from me, I received countless life lessons in attitude. The ones who thrived appeared to possess some essential form of resilience. They clearly had their struggles to contend with, but they were not downtrodden. Somehow, these individuals had come to a place within themselves where they could wear that heavy yoke of routine physical misery. It's nothing anyone would ever learn to like, but the resilient ones seemed to regard the procedure as being akin to stopping in to have their car serviced so it can move on down the road. It's not possible to lie to yourself about the situation when you have to show up and ride the filter system on a regular basis. All you have is attitude, the way you insist on relating to the cards in your hand.

I saw the truth of it: how tiny course corrections to one's attitude, administered throughout the day, have enough collective power to completely change your experience.

Patients came in three times a week for at least three hours, maybe four. Some then went off to work while others were too sick to hold a job and had to battle boredom and the creeping sense of uselessness that haunts any long-term patient.

Treating people in such difficult circumstances, I tried to combine smooth, deft treatment with a positive and attentive attitude. I'm sure they all appreciated that, but some were either too ill or too depressed to engage with me about much of anything beyond the required discussion of the process.

Others, however, could and would relate to me in a revealing manner. I was especially glad for the emotional experience provided by this difficult job when I did my own time in the hospitals of Boston and Houston and in recovery at home. I believe that the more you know about the ways others handle their difficulties, the better prepared you can be to carry your own.

Although the dialysis job helped cover the bills, the brutal hours made me think twice about it as a long-term job, so I transferred my college credits to a community college to finish my required classes. This would put me in a position to get into nursing school later, and dialysis work could be a fallback position if I needed work while looking for a job after graduation.

Given those hours and with a little boy at home, I had almost no time for a social life, but that didn't stop me from trying to have one. I dated a lot, but since I never wanted to get close to anyone, it was always very hollow. I didn't mind the dating part but settling down was something I didn't want any part of. Fortunately, I had been friends with Karah, my cousin by marriage, even before Tim and Mom were wed, and she also worked at the dialysis center. So she knew firsthand how difficult our work/life balance truly was.

We tried to still socialize on weekends outside of work, and if we couldn't, we talked on the phone. We would be exhausted but still managed to stay up chatting into the night until our alarms were ready to go off for work at three in the morning. My life had no balance. There were not enough hours in the day to do everything I wanted. Karah was one of the only people who truly understood that.

Noah made it all worthwhile, though. He was a bundle of energy who seemed to delight in living. At this point in his life, Mom and Dad were such a strong addition of love and support that I believe he felt secure in his home.

Having a child imposed a level of maturity on me that I was glad to embrace. Simply holding him and drinking in his presence, knowing that his life and future were in my hands, convicted me that I had to do right by him.

Since I had the wonderful luxury of Noah's loving grand-parents to back me up with babysitting, I pushed myself to work hard while he was too small to miss me in hopes I could secure a better job with better hours before he got older. I wanted to do more than cover the bills. I wanted to prepare to take a major step up in our lives within the next few years. Whenever I heard the phrase "God helps those who help themselves," it always sounded true. I followed it like a beacon, and it worked well—for a while.

As you may have already screamed at the page, I forgot all about the wisdom of moderation.

Then early one morning I was driving on a narrow and unlit stretch of interstate between my house and the dialysis clinic when a deer jumped out in front of my car. I realize it's pretty unlikely that the creature did a deliberate swan dive out of the bushes and into my path, but it sure looked that way at the time.

Perhaps if I had been less fatigued, my reactions would have been faster. As it was, I responded with groggy reflexes that were not up to the challenge. Before I could hit the brakes or swerve, there was a terrible crash and an impact that felt like hitting a wall.

The deer was killed right away. Its body flew up over the hood and into the windshield, where it bashed through the glass antlers first. I instinctively threw up my arms at the moment of impact, and they were in that position when one of the antlers pierced my wrist.

The car flipped over and ran into a deep ditch, and I was knocked unconscious when my head struck the driver's side door. The backseat was totally gone.

It was just as well that I wasn't conscious, because rescue was unlikely and the panic would have been bad. It was around four in the morning on a lightly used section of highway, and in order for anyone to help, they had to see my car down in that dark ditch. Rescue wasn't likely to come from anyone driving a car.

But soon a large truck came along, and the driver's seat was high enough off the ground that he could see down into the ditch. He spotted my car and called for help.

When I came around, I was trapped in my seat by the wreckage, staring a dead deer in the face and feeling the pressure and pain of my right wrist.

It seemed like forever before help came, although it was probably only around fifteen or twenty minutes before EMTs arrived with an ambulance. They covered me with a tarp for protection and cut me free. Once that was done, they put a neck brace on me, lifted me onto a gurney, and transported me to the University of Louisville Hospital. I received treatment for the next several hours.

Six bones were broken in my back, and my neck was sprained. The wrist puncture was clean enough that they used surgical glue instead of stitches to hold it together. The doctors assured me that if I had not been wearing my seat belt, I would have died.

The follow-up was two weeks of bed rest. Since Noah was still a toddler then, you can imagine how well this all went over.

---

I make it a firm policy that when God pins me to the driver's seat with deer antlers, I give him my full attention. There was no longer any doubt that I had to find some way to trust in the Lord that would allow me to ease up on the throttle. That simple lesson had just been beyond me, until then. Happily, this time my slow spiritual learning process actually kept up with the challenge.

I am *so* grateful Noah was at my mom's house when I hit the deer. As I've said, I don't claim to know how much God intervenes in everyday affairs. There is always the issue of free will. I know I consider it a true blessing that Noah was with my parents instead of with me when the crash took place.

My mother later pointed out that I set myself up for it, trying so hard that I was sure to crash somewhere, whether it was a literal crash or some other form of self-made disaster. My cousin Karah was less blunt about it but seemed to share the opinion. I had been clinging to my inner tension like someone who has grabbed a live wire and can't make their muscles let go. Reality had to pin me down to stop me.

It worked. With those six broken bones in my back, I had to move slow and wear a brace around my neck for a few weeks, but it's hard to look back on that relatively easy recovery and complain, now that I have a visceral understanding of how lethal a collision like that can be.

I rededicated my life to Christ, not because my devotion had been insincere but because I realized I was being willful and trying to fix everything myself. And just making a prayerful proclamation wasn't going to do it. I needed to trust God enough to release that constantly coiled spring. For the next two years, I was able to take care of my little boy and myself and also make regular time to be still inside and know the Lord. As a result, a far deeper sense of personal quiet came into my life. It added to my relationship with Noah as well.

By the time I was twenty-four, my parents had moved to Texas. The first time I went for a visit I loved it there (in spite of the humidity). So just as a lark, I put in a job application at a corporate housing firm there. I had come to feel too emotionally involved with the patients in dialysis, and so

I had found work in the sales and marketing field instead. The company in Texas offered me the job, and the timing was good. Noah and I soon moved.

Life in Texas immediately felt right, and I was in good emotional shape. However, I was about to get a hard lesson in situational awareness. One evening shortly after arriving, I was out driving with Noah and we stopped at a market for a few necessities. Being new to the area, I didn't realize the neighborhood was sketchy and not the best place for a woman alone with a child to be. We did our shopping and walked back out to the car. By now it was well after dark, and the semilighted parking lot didn't offer much security.

My little boy was still in the seat of the grocery cart as I bent to the trunk to load some of the bags. Just as I bent over, I felt the tip of a gun barrel jam into my back.

This was a first. A powerful primal instinct left me no doubt as to what it was, but it had nothing to offer me after that, since the fight-or-flight mode was no good. I couldn't fight an armed man, and with Noah there I couldn't run.

I slowly turned to face a solitary male about my own age, ordinary looking except for his level of desperation. He was either a drug addict in need of a fix or the most nervous man I'd ever come across. Somehow, his fidgety loitering had gone unnoticed by everyone in the area until now. And now it was noticed only by me and Noah. Nobody else was around. Whatever happened next, there would be no cavalry in time to help us.

He demanded money. The gun was persuasive.

He must have been lying in wait for the perfect victim and then took advantage of the fact that there weren't other people in that part of the lot. I've never experienced telepathy, but for some reason it was clear that he was doing something he had practiced before and that he expected me to cry out or scream. He really did look poised to shoot me, grab my bag, and run.

I looked him in the eyes and quietly said, "Here's my purse. There's nothing in the car. Please just take what you need without saying anything to my little boy about what's going on."

An instant of confusion flashed across his face before he could conceal it. I imagine he wasn't prepared for that response. He took the purse from me and pulled out the cash, then tossed it down and hurried away.

Noah was only four, but very little escaped him. After I retrieved my purse and hurried back to the grocery cart, the first thing he did was ask me why that man took our money. So much for keeping him out of it.

I just replied that that man really needed money right now and sometimes you have to help people out. He searched my face and seemed to accept the answer, so we got out of there.

The unfortunate timing of the robbery was that I had cashed my last paycheck from my old job and was carrying three hundred dollars to parse out on expenses until I got my first paycheck from my new job, which was unfortunate because Noah and I had rented a house just shortly before. So while I could report the crime, which I did, and they could apprehend the thief, which they later did, there was nothing to be done for the financial squeeze.

I can't explain my calmness that night. My assurance that the Lord was with me allowed me to be calm in that parking lot, and I believe my state infected the perpetrator. Yes, some might say it was blind luck that protected us. God may have had nothing to do with it at all. My experience is simply that the more I make room for God in my life, the "luckier" I get.

———

So there we were, four-year-old Noah and I, trying to find our way as a little family. I'm sure every parent who is going it alone knows the desire to find a great partner, unless they just prefer not to get into a relationship at all. I wanted Noah to have a complete family. I had seen my grandparents happily in love for over fifty years. I knew that type of happiness existed. I just hadn't found it yet. But no amount of emotional need ever seemed to be enough to persuade me to fully trust any of the young men I happened to date. It really wasn't them; it was me. I always ended up running away the moment anything got serious.

I kept telling myself that Noah and I could get through life just fine. But I hated to think of what that would actually mean.

The only cure I know for excessive anxiety over the future is a conscious decision to believe that God has a bigger plan for my life. I hope it goes without saying that this is far easier to talk about doing than to live out from one day to the next.

Staying spiritually centered became a full-time job in the months that followed. But I stayed with it, and it paid back in the form of a healthier outlook, plus a more peaceful and accepting state of mind. I knew how hard it was to be a single mom. But I could see a future for us now.

By now you already know that I'm not going to claim the Lord prepared me for the Boston Marathon bombing and everything that followed by steering me into my prior experiences working in the medical field and enduring countless hospital visits. I also won't argue with those who call it a happy coincidence. But I tell you, when it came to swallowing my panic in that Boston hospital, my knowledge of the medical field played a big part in quelling my anxiety. I felt familiar with a lot of what went on around me. The surgical setting and the rash of operations were a bit less intimidating too when I could visualize what was going on with what was left of me. I also found that I never felt like complaining about the number of needles that pierced my skin daily, considering the huge needles I had been required to put into the arms of my dialysis patients.

Me when I was about two years old.

My grandparents have always been my favorite people. They are the reason I believe in love and the two people who pushed me to keep writing throughout my life. They would have been the first people to buy my book. I miss them terribly.

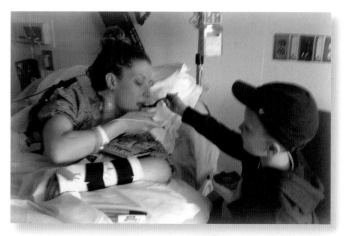

When Noah came to visit me the first time, I had no appetite, but he was determined to help me eat. I finished every bite.

Noah was just learning to write and signed my cast.

Me with my second external fixator. My face says it all here.

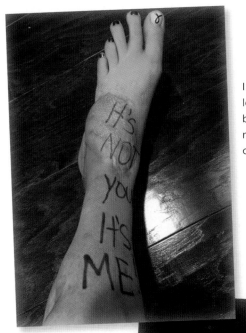

I joked that my leg was like a "bad boyfriend" that I needed to get out of my life.

I thought waking up without half of my leg would scare me, but I had never felt so relieved. My nurse drew a smiley face and left a note.

I decided I'd never be ashamed of the amputation. Neither the bombing nor the amputation define who I am.

My mom and I after several surgeries. She was by my side every day and has always been my biggest supporter.

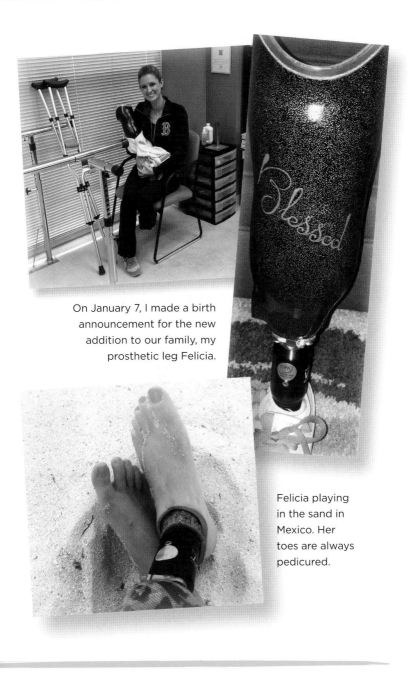

On January 7, I made a birth announcement for the new addition to our family, my prosthetic leg Felicia.

Felicia playing in the sand in Mexico. Her toes are always pedicured.

In July 2015, I was asked by the Houston Astros to throw out the first pitch at their opening game against the Boston Red Sox.

My nurses from Boston, Tracy and Naomi, came to visit me in Texas.

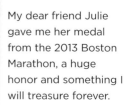

My dear friend Julie gave me her medal from the 2013 Boston Marathon, a huge honor and something I will treasure forever.

Ten years apart
only made the bond
stronger when Chris
and I met again.

On our
wedding day
and the
start of a
beautiful
new chapter
in our lives.

Holding Ryleigh for the first time. The joy I felt in those few minutes can never be put into words.

Our first family photo, when we could finally bring Ryleigh home at last. Life had never felt more complete.

# -10-

# Silent Explosion

Oddly enough, it was only after the chaos of the terror attacks and the intensity of life in the hospital had subsided that the darkest shadow fell over me. This obstacle, by its nature, was concealed.

Beyond the effects of my physical injuries, I had a long uphill slog with PTSD. I had been counseled about its potential effects, but I was still caught off guard when it metastasized into my everyday thinking, long after the ride home from the hospital. It's only after having felt the strength, subtlety, and perseverance of PTSD that I came to a real understanding of what it is and why it can be so devastating to the lives of survivors. It has no respect for strength or for weakness, for age or for gender.

I began avoiding risk and seeking safety in countless little ways. I didn't connect the dots. And I never gave any thought to the idea of PTSD having a negative effect on my spiritual life. But it did, and for a while it darkened my outlook of a bigger plan.

During my alone times, when the house got quiet, a pallor of fear descended over me and ruined my attempts to visualize any sort of workable future for us. Noah seemed to have an innate understanding of the situation, whether just from his compassionate nature or our shared experience with this thing, and his patience with my limitations was endless.

Since I was of no use in getting him outside to break up the scenery, I encouraged him to go out for small excursions with other family members. At home, he would sit with me while we planned activities for when I could finally move around again. We both needed those planning sessions. No matter how bad the PTSD got or how intense my anxiety attacks proved to be, I was so thankful there was never a break in my connection with my little boy.

My dependency during that early recovery was the hardest part for me, beyond all the physical pain. I don't say that lightly, because pain at that level can drive you to complete distraction and poison everything else. But the slow drip of embarrassment or even humiliation at asking family members for the most basic of assistance tends to wear a person down. Even when you can avoid the immediate panic of finding yourself in a helpless situation, as I did, there is the seeping effect, the grinding down of the ego.

I did my best to relax into the pull of this giant whirlpool. There was no way to fight the current.

Here I was at the age of twenty-six, having raised my little boy for the past five years. We had been an independent little family, making our way well enough, until the bombs went off. Now we were back at my parents' house. Noah was making it his mission to cheer up his invalid mother, and I was pushing my recovery to get myself back to my role as his caretaker, not his handicapped mom.

Everyone encouraged me to take the recovery slowly and not try to swallow the whole thing at once. I realized it was good advice, but it was hard to put into practice. I want to trust God's plan for me, even when I can't see and can't prove it. The bombs changed none of that. But the trauma set a cancer growing in me. Even though it wouldn't show up on a hospital scan, it made itself known by its unhealthy symptoms. They were subtle at first, casting shadows that slowly deepened. I started making choices about my future that I would have hesitated to make from a more centered state of mind.

I have no other explanation for the return of the Obedient Preacher's Daughter. I had thought she had been laid out on a slab for good. It was as if some bone-deep level of fear got blasted into me along with the shrapnel and revived the insecurities that had created that side of my personality.

And, of course, the OPD syndrome was only part of it. I was about to begin learning the recovery dance. Lots of injured people know it. It starts with the familiar old three steps forward, two steps back. But you quickly learn to be thankful when it's only two steps back and not ten.

For several months before the Boston Marathon, I had been in a long-distance relationship with my boyfriend, traveling between Houston, Texas, and Rochester, New York. We had been at the marathon with a bunch of his relatives and he was also impacted by the blast, but with far less severe injuries.

While I was still in the hospital, there had been some press interest in us as a couple, and six months after the bombing took place, he traveled to Houston and surprised me by proposing marriage. The media caught wind of it, and everything took off from there.

I don't know why he did that, and I don't know why I accepted, especially with my history of running away from anything serious. We hardly knew each other, and while I thought we were compatible in terms of our faith and our spiritual lives, there were way too many unanswered questions about issues that mattered.

Maybe we both thought it was meant to be, not so much because of our personal chemistry but because we had survived. Gratitude is a powerful emotion. The truth is that we didn't have what it takes to be married. But unfortunately, as soon as the first inklings of our engagement broke on social media, interest in our story spiked, and suddenly the wave of attention was a flash flood.

My mother made it clear she wasn't happy with the way things were developing, but she respected my independence. I'd like to think I would have come to my senses on my own if things had slowed down a little, but instead, a major bridal website called and offered a huge fantasy wedding in return for the photo and publicity rights to the whole event.

Because I was new to the public eye, it seemed as if this was all some sort of fantasy and not the valuable media event that it actually was. Six months after we became engaged, we were married. The location was the Biltmore Estates in Asheville, North Carolina. The place is spectacular and has a compelling romantic aura. My fiancé seemed to warm right up to the attention, and although I had a hard time smiling for the camera between my leg pain and my self-consciousness, I did as expected. My OPD syndrome was flying on this.

The wedding was gorgeous, everything they had promised. I was up on a temporary prosthetic for the first time, a leg crutch that enabled me to walk on my knee and take the pressure off my lower left leg, walking between giant floral arches on a carpet of flower petals. It was an overwhelming scene, fit for minor royalty. Everything looked the way it was supposed to look, a fairy-tale wedding for two miracle survivors.

What actually happened was that another bomb went off, but this one was the kind that makes no noise. Instead, it silently blows everything to pieces in slow motion.

As events built up to the ceremony, I considered the knot in my stomach to be a sign of nerves. I had never been a public person, and the intensity of the setting was enough to drop your jaw in itself. But now I look back in hindsight and see the warning signs flashing away. Isn't it strange how our minds can edit out so much of whatever stands right before us?

My new husband had a lot of friends.

At the wedding rehearsal dinner the night before, one of them ran up to him and leaped onto him, with her arms thrown around his neck and her legs wrapped tight around his thighs. She just hung there, like her tiny dress was made of Velcro.

There are those moments in all of our lives when we glimpse a single image that tells us a whole fistful of stories. This was one. But I was busy telling myself that the feeling of *wrong wrong wrong* in my stomach was nerves. It might have been nerves. Maybe it was just nerves.

After all, as I repeated to myself, we both came from strong Christian homes. We shared so many values. It seemed to me that the thing to do was focus my optimism and positive energy on making this marriage work. I had brought this man into my son's life, and there was no way to pretend that this was a decision that affected only me.

*Part Four*

# *The* WHIRLWIND

# -11-

# The Many-Headed Media

Not long after I got home from the hospital, I came out of the media cocoon that had protected me up to that point. It was a rude awakening. Internet haters and paranoiacs had begun to circulate rumors that the bombing had been a hoax. Surprise, it was all fake. All those victims were either lying or else they never existed.

The race officials were lying, the bystanders and witnesses were lying, the press was lying, the police were lying, and the entire staff of every hospital in Boston was up to their necks in the deception. They had to be; there is no other way to pull off a hoax of this proportion.

I have to step back from the personal anger and indignation I feel when I think of this so I can calmly ask how even the most bitter internet troll could believe that this whole thing could be successfully done in an age when our own government and our biggest corporations can't keep secrets to save their lives. But somehow or other, the haters managed to believe it had all been hushed up when it came to the Boston Marathon bombing.

Somebody reproduced a reversed photo of me to *prove* that my injuries were a hoax. "See? Her injury changed legs!" They did this as if nobody has ever noticed what happens when you digitally flip a photograph. Whatever drove their great need to expose this "hoax," they had no time to consider the obvious. On the internet, we can all post things and forget that there is an actual human being on the receiving end.

The nicest thing I was called was an "actress," but some went on to claim that my hunger for fame was so intense that I blew my own leg off to get attention and win acting jobs.

I don't consider myself a naïve person just because I do my best to remain civil with other people, but this was the first time I personally encountered strangers who chose to speak the most vile things their imaginations could conjure—always expressed through the safety of an internet connection, of course. While I suspect there are legitimate issues of mental illness and borderline personalities here, the whole picture comports with my idea of the kind of behavior that any of us is capable of sliding into if we come under the wrong influences and are without an internal compass.

Having stood on the receiving end of that form of public mania, I came to believe that the articles had the effect of engaging cogs and wheels in the minds of certain people and setting them spinning. With these people, I believe that kinks in their worldview just happened to fit the details of my story, thus turning the lock on the lid to Pandora's box and releasing a swirl of angry bats. These are unedited samples from Facebook and other social media:

You are such a lying, treasonous pig! You stole and lied to the good people of America. You need to be in prison with the rest of your crisis acting friends. One day, you will have to answer to God. You better live it up while you can because he is a just God. I feel sorry for that little boy. I can't imagine having a mother that lies and steals from her neighbors and betrays her country. You are such a pathetic human. It must be sad to look in the mirror. May God have mercy on you.

You are going to rot in hell for your lies. Enjoy your millions of dollars while you can. You won't be able to take that with you when you face Satan for eternity.

It's obvious that your leg is there and you are just good at photo shop. Why don't you quit hiding it behind your computer and come out and tell the world you're nothing but a stupid blonde fake.

Every day I am spending the time it takes to expose you and the other "survivors" for the liars that you are. One day you will pay for this and I hope to be in the front row when it happens.

I bet you were really pretty before you injured yourself and almost took your own life to get attention.

Whore.

Could there be a more absolutely obvious hoaxer in this universe than the Boston Smoke Bombing Hoax's Rebekah Gregory?

There's a phrase for you: "the Boston Smoke Bombing Hoax's Rebekah Gregory." Lovely. Think of the sort of emotional pain a person has to be in to put their energy behind baseless accusations directed at not just me but so many others who were there and who are strangers. A person who was at least clever enough to come up with such a nasty quip might also come up with a way out of their own painful situation, if only their energy were turned in a healthy direction.

There is a toxic river of this online, a mile wide and a quarter inch deep. I realize the internet is a place where people are much more free to display their illness and rage. But I have to confess that the sheer ferocity of it was stunning. It knocked me back.

Fortunately, my childhood had made me familiar with people who pronounce truths with cosmic certainty, eyes blazing with confidence. I recognize the essence of their fiery passion and the rock-solid "certainties" they represent. I already know that such people cling to their fantasies with white knuckles.

So the haters were at my digital doorstep. What they couldn't have known was that I'd been studying the topic since I was a child. It didn't make it any easier to deal with, but it also didn't make it as shocking to see people act in such a manner. And while nobody likes reading posts intended to inflame them, I feel that I can do it more easily when I remind myself that the media whirlwind doesn't matter to the heart of my story anyway, whether it blows in my favor or not.

I also know that I put myself out there for the people who may need it. Not the haters. Does this mean everyone will accept me with open arms? Definitely not. And that is one of the biggest things I've had to overcome. I have been a people pleaser all my life, after all. But I do believe that there are still far more good people in the world than there are bad.

And after making a few futile attempts to defend myself, I quickly realized that trying to "dialogue" with the bad ones was a waste of time. I would much rather spend my energy focusing on the good.

After all, so many more expressions of kindness were sent my way by complete strangers, people who wanted nothing more than to give me a mental boost and a thumbs-up. Their responses gave me a glimpse of how much good there really is and how much decency remains alive and well out there.

My life had been quiet before the attacks. Nothing in my past prepared me to be on the public stage. While I was still in the hospital, I didn't realize how well my single-patient room protected me from the problem of feeling overwhelmed in large spaces and among crowds. Even with the constant flow of orderlies, nurses, and doctors through my room, there were seldom more than two or three others with me at one time, including my mother.

Now that I was home, I often referred back to the time I experienced my first true panic attack, which happened when my physical therapist took me outside the hospital for my first breath of fresh air since the bombing. Even though I knew the essential signs of a panic attack, the deceptive nature of my PTSD changed my thinking. It made everything I knew about anxiety seem completely wrong and not to be trusted, for reasons I wouldn't have been able to explain.

It was as if the disorder somehow distorted my thinking so that none of my usual defenses against personal fear were effective. They didn't do a thing to immunize me once my heartbeat jumped up and I felt that powerful rush of tension go through all my muscles. When the first one hit, it caused my body to clench so tightly that I was vibrating in my wheelchair. My stomach twisted and the air suddenly felt as if it didn't contain enough oxygen. I started pulling in great breaths of air but still didn't feel I was taking a decent breath.

Mom tried to tell me I was suffering from anxiety or panic disorder or whatever you want to call it. I didn't think she was wrong about that, but I absolutely could not make myself take in the information. My anxiety blocked out logic and reason and just left me gasping until we were safely back inside and in my room.

---

The public whirlwind, the glorious wedding venue, and the image of my new husband and me as the Happy Ending Couple came at us from all directions. He seemed to love the attention, but under the circumstances I was uncomfortable in the spotlight. The PTSD was starting to give me real anxieties, especially whenever I was around a lot of people.

By then I had also begun to itch with traces of real concern over the state of our relationship. The problem for me was that when you're in the story, you can't see the story. That means you can't guarantee the ending—in a situation where the guaranteed ending is of the essence.

I held silent pep talks with my hesitant self, trying to work out the real cause of my concern. But blind spots being the way they are, the answer was in front of me and I looked right through it.

Each time I began to openly doubt this marriage, a flood of guilt washed over me for being so ungrateful. Why, not only had I survived the bombing but so had he. Beyond all of this good fortune, we had been so generously provided with this unbelievable wedding in return for nothing more than the photo rights. This was a fairy tale come true for a fairy-tale relationship and a fairy-tale wedding. Did I just use the term *fairy tale* three times in a row? Oops, that was four . . .

Of course, I was dazzled by everything that was done for us. I struggled to avoid letting the experience get poisoned by my own old issues or old memories. They contained those old lies that assured me I didn't deserve any of what was happening. I thought this internal struggle was the reason for my persistent sense of dread. It felt like a faint stomachache that sat just on the borderline of my perception.

Up to a point, I was able to use plain logic to find my way out of these judgment traps. Most times, I could remind myself that getting blown up doesn't mean you "deserve" public affection or support. So what you do, then, is find the grace to accept such blessings when they do come and be glad for them.

That worked, on the plain self-talk level. But where my spirit got stuck was on that faint stomachache, that nagging sense of dis-ease within all the public attention. It was so well intended, by such sincere and generous people, but I got stuck on the concern over its potential effect on our marriage. My very good-looking new husband was idolized by many lovely young women who were all openly fascinated with his status as a terrorism survivor.

In truth, I saw everything I needed to see in order to predict the weather on this. I knew everything I needed to know to recognize that the setting was fabulous but the play was wrong.

Missed it.

I felt somehow that I owed this fairy-tale wedding and the happy ending it represented to my family and friends and to all of our support system. Nobody is guilty of telling me that whopper either. I bought into it on my own.

How symmetrical it was; we were public darlings because our dream wedding was the perfect antidote to the awfulness everyone felt in the aftermath of the attacks. *How ungrateful was I to question all that?* An internal voice asked me that again and again.

The torment drove my choices more strongly than I realized, and I failed to truly, honestly place my trust in God and stayed in the fearful place instead. Had I been in a clearer state of mind, free from pain medication, constant surgery, and of course the media, I would have been able to accept the possibility that this marriage was already deeply threatened.

I used logic to tell myself that lightning wasn't going to strike me again so soon. How could it? I was safe enough for the time being, right? I later learned this is called "magical thinking," and it includes any idea that pretends misfortune is on some sort of timetable or that evil is subject to principles of fairness.

So my failing was that instead of bringing the real situation to light, I dusted off the old mask of Obedient Preacher's Daughter. She could smile at her own execution.

# -12-

# Losing Weight on the Wax Fruit Diet

After the glow of the public spotlight, my husband and I moved into our new home together and life was supposed to be fine. It was as photogenic as a beautiful bowl of wax fruit, the kind that makes your mouth water because it is so perfectly made. It was everything you could ever want in a bowl of fruit—except for actual fruit.

My mother sensed my restlessness but kindly withheld her observations. Instead, she focused her attention on my life outside the home. She pointed out that I needed to carefully consider the best way to respond to the spiritual hunger that people began to show around me in public. There were certain to be more encounters with people who were genuine and sincere in wanting to learn something from me. They deserved more than whatever I could come up with off the top of my head when we encountered each other. And there were so many times when I was in too much pain from moving around to be able to calmly consider a compelling question right there on the spot. I needed to think things through and be ready when the time came to articulate my thoughts so I could do it whether or not I was in the right mood at any given time for encountering a questioning stranger.

So many people ask me "how" one survives such trauma. Maybe they are looking for a way to immunize themselves or learn that one piece of information they might use to save themselves if they ever get caught in a brutal public attack. As you see, that's dicey territory for a casual conversation. Though I want to extend a sincere and well-considered reply in such a situation, I know better than to presume to solve other people's inner problems through a single public encounter. I can't solve anything, anyway. I can only point them in the direction of the One who can. So the question became: How much detail does such a moment need?

On occasions when I have time to talk to someone on a deeper level, I can describe the awareness that allows me to experience God's grace and find peace. But in those encounters I am also honest about the times when I was offered grace and simply didn't see it. Or when I got caught up in worldly struggles to the point that I lost sight of what I can only describe as the bigness underneath all the smallness.

My prosthetic leg often draws attention in public, and sometimes people then recognize my face from news photos. I'm glad to say there have been some wonderful and deeply moving encounters that have spontaneously come up in this way.

When I meet people in this fashion, I never know what they believe about the big picture, unless they bring it up, but I often sense the spiritual hunger in their stories. In those moments, I do my best to relate to them as one who knows my own flaws. I let them know that I live in gratitude for the love of Christ, because it guides me away from hurtful thoughts, whether those thoughts are my own or from others.

Each of these encounters sets off a spark inside me, an urge to do more for others and to always be as kind to the people I meet as these strangers have been to me. That constant reminder allows me to see the bigger picture, no matter how grim the weather might be at the time.

The fairy-tale marriage didn't work from the beginning. Blunt people have asked me why two Christians dedicated to their spiritual well-being could allow that to happen. After all, we made such a pretty package. Here it is: for two people to be married, they both have to be married. The marriage turned out to not be functional, and I will spare readers further details.

My part in the dysfunction was to sit in my imaginary backyard tree and keep my head down because I couldn't find the strength to trust God to get me through my failed "dream marriage." I had no idea what to tell people when they asked how everything was going. It took awhile before I could piece out a reasonable answer.

At those times, I was so grateful for the accepting nature of some people online. They may have been strangers, but I believe their positive effect on me and on the situation was real. They are the opposite of the internet trolls.

My sense of failure in that brief marriage made my recovery seem to drag on. I felt life passing me by. In dark moments, I sometimes found myself wondering why I had survived. Here I was, home for recovery and many months past the bombing, but it certainly didn't feel as if I was doing much with this second chance of mine. I surely wasn't contributing to society.

The response to my prayers for purpose was not a blinding light of revelation. It was the simple realization that nobody said I had to wait until I was walking again to do something for others and boost my self-esteem in the bargain.

Interest in my Facebook page, which I had started in September 2013, quickly expanded and spread. When I saw the scope of outreach that was suddenly available through that platform, it was plain to me that I was able to shine a light for others there, in spite of operating the page with only a semimobile body.

It felt like a cloud passing away from the sun. I wondered what had taken me so long to do this.

———

This is how I came to know Kylee, who also lived in Texas, a couple hundred miles from my mom's home. Kylee's mother reached out to me on Facebook because she was feeling desperate for a source of hope for her struggling daughter. She was searching for answers on the girl's behalf, because Kylee had recently been in a critical ATV accident. She had suffered devastating injuries to her leg, and it was so mangled that she had to endure many surgeries in the attempt to save it. The results were not good. And so now, at the age of fourteen, Kylee and her mom were facing tough decisions about the course of her medical treatment.

Her story touched my heart. Not only did I understand her medical dilemma and her fight to save her leg but I also thought of myself in high school at the age of fourteen. I remembered wanting so badly to blend in while instead my frequent dizzy spells made me stick out in embarrassing ways. Kylee only wanted to be accepted and live a normal teenage life.

Her biggest obstacle was trying to get her head around the medical transition from staying strong and fighting the good fight to keep her leg to facing the reality of her situation. There simply had not been anywhere near the level of recuperation necessary to heal her leg or to regain natural movement.

That first night I spoke with her mom on the phone for hours. She told me what they were going through with Kylee's emotional struggle to recuperate, and I described my version of the same struggle. I could see how hard they were trying to manage Kylee's situation, but they had fewer support resources than those available to me and felt overwhelmed by the choices ahead of them.

There is a terrible burden of false guilt that I believe many people suffer from when they are trying to recover from grievous wounds, or when they love someone who is. They carry a certain sense of obligation after being spared from something worse. But in spite of it, they feel ashamed of how difficult it is to remain grateful simply because the damage done to them weighs heavily on them.

Gratitude tells us to accept, accept. Meanwhile, pain demands that we do something, do something. Pain can be a real gratitude killer.

Then Kylee's mom mentioned that her daughter was having a birthday in a few weeks. I asked her if I could surprise Kylee with a visit. Her mom was overjoyed, and her happiness did me good. I can assure you that after so many months of having to be self-centered all the time, it felt wonderful to be giving back a small fraction of what had been given to me. I felt the truth of a gift's value to the giver.

A second external fixator had just been removed from my leg when I went to see her. This was fortuitous, since Kylee was currently deciding between getting her own "medieval" fixator device or enduring yet another operation, which her doctor didn't want her to do.

So I found myself wheeling through the airport with a left leg still too weak to walk on, even after the second fixator, boarding a plane on crutches and pain meds, and setting off to Dallas. Her family had arranged to pick me up at the airport and drive me to their little town.

It took a leap of faith to set out on this trip, since these people were complete strangers to me. The idea made my mom extremely nervous. But I believe that when God's hand is in something, you will just feel that it's the right direction for you to take. And, of course, Kylee's mother also had to take the same leap of faith, since they didn't know me either.

When we all finally met, Kylee and I both cried. There were a lot of tears over those few days. I opened up to her about the fears and insecurities I faced in my early recovery, as well as my ongoing struggle with those same things. I opened up about my physical pain and emotional anxieties for the future.

I think Kylee may have been expecting me to preach at her as an "expert" on this treatment. She seemed so relieved to find a sister in suffering, not a lecturer who came to tell her what she was supposed to feel and think and do. A strong sense of rapport quickly grew between us, and a beautiful relationship blossomed.

Kylee saw firsthand what the fixator did, with no sugar-coating over the ordeal for the patient, but she also got a clear picture of the potential outcome and was able to discuss it with me at length. I don't doubt that the descriptions of long screws sticking out of my leg gave my words extra force with her.

Naturally, she still looked upon the procedure with a healthy amount of dread, but now she had seen a pathway to potential healing. I was still there visiting with her when I saw her make the mental leap necessary to take on the long and difficult process.

The final ingredient was her love of the game. Kylee was an avid soccer player, and despite her injuries she desperately wanted to get back out on the field. So while I was still with her that weekend, I made her a promise that if she would try the fixator as her doctor wanted her to, I would make it a point to be there, cheering her on from the front row, once she had recovered enough to play soccer again. And I assured her that I felt certain this would happen for her, sooner than she thought.

With that image in mind, Kylee agreed and scheduled the operation to attach the painful device. She understood there would be a mountain of discomfort ahead before the fixator could be removed.

But once she was into it, she stayed with the process. Two years after our first meeting, I went back to Hallsville, Texas, to cheer Kylee on in the soccer game we had both envisioned for her. (It also happened to fall on her seventeenth birthday.)

As much as I helped Kylee, she also helped me. I believe there are few things that will speed your healing like helping someone else to heal. At the same time you are giving reinforcement to them, you are also demonstrating to yourself that you have enough energy to give to others. Even though you are still recovering, you are in a state of abundance sufficient to help others and reassure yourself that in time, you will heal too.

It was shortly after the Boston explosions that my co-workers stepped in, out of the kindness of their hearts, and set up a GoFundMe account for me. Since I had no idea what expenses I was going to incur with insurance deductibles and co-pays, as well as mounting home expenses until I could work again, I was grateful that this was done by such kind people.

When people donated money to the site, they sometimes left a little note of encouragement. Mom and I started making a habit of checking to see what people were saying in order to make a list and send them thank-you cards.

But cards were going in both directions. I received a note from Amanda, who lived in Houston. She and her family had heard about my situation, and she had empathy for me. She told me that her ten-year-old little boy, Braden, was in the hospital at the time, fighting an aggressive form of cancer.

It was heartbreaking to picture what it would be like for me, for our whole family, if that were Noah. Even though my little boy went through something so horrific, he was a miracle who more or less walked away. This poor mom couldn't say that for her son. But in spite of her pain, she was soldiering on for him.

Amanda briefly described Braden's strong sense of his own spiritual life. He had confided to her that he experienced an encounter with God. During this encounter, he heard God tell him to give his birthday money to a bombing victim, to help them get a new leg. Braden's parents were astonished to hear this from their ten-year-old. But they respected his wishes and began looking up victims to find the right one to give the money to.

They came across me, a blast victim from their hometown. And while the obvious tie was that we lived in the same area, Amanda told me her heart went out to me because of my position as a single mom. She had been a single mom until she met her husband, who later adopted Braden.

This little boy's selflessness and personal maturity stunned me. There he was, facing down a terrible illness filled with miserable experiences, and his compassion was evident. It brought me back to my own experience years earlier, meeting that young girl in the hospital elevator who displayed such an example of gratitude and humility.

I was anxious to meet Braden when I got out of the hospital. I wanted to hug him and thank him. The meeting itself was nothing short of an encounter with one of

God's gentle messengers in this world: a good boy with a heart to match.

Now, three years later, I still have a strong friendship with Braden and his family, and I am so happy to say that he is in remission from his cancer.

# -13-

# It's Not You, It's Me

It took a year and a half after the explosion to work through all the surgical interventions in the attempt to save my ruined left leg. Everything the surgeons did helped, but none of it was enough to restore that limb. My body was still trying to adapt to all the shrapnel I still carried, and my system just couldn't seem to find enough strength and healing power to get my ruined leg back into usable shape. And in spite of all the complex surgeries, I still didn't have enough of my leg left for it to function normally again.

I had also grown about as weary as I could be with the process of going under general anesthesia and then sitting through another long healing process for the surgical wounds. At this point, they had slipped that gas mask over my face and sent me off to sleep seventeen times. I had come to dread the entire process.

So now I was back in the hospital to have my eighteenth operation, but this time I intended for it to be the last of the series. I had accepted that amputation was the only alternative to the never-ending drag of surgeries and recovery. As disappointing as it was to make that decision, there was also real relief in it.

The night before, the lovely Edd Hendee and his wife, Nina, hosted our family at a restaurant they own in Houston, and we held a family good-bye party for my leg. I had my "Boston Strong" manicure and pedicure, which meant I was going to go under the knife rocking the toenails I would keep as well as the ones I would be losing.

I wrote my "breakup letter" to my leg and posted it online, then used a marker to write across my soon-to-be departed lower limb, "It's not you, it's me." It was just time, that's all. I joked that it was like a bad boyfriend and I needed to get it out of my life.

By this time, I had been interviewed by media reporters on several occasions when they did articles that included interviews with Boston survivors and their families. Unfortunately, the articles were always accompanied by the gory photos. Whenever I saw them, my empathy for those people and my memory of the pain flashed through me like a wave of fire.

Most people were sympathetic in their comments and feedback, and numerous celebrities were kind enough to have me on their shows and let me celebrate this long road of survival. But the inevitable haters went from claiming the whole attack was a hoax to leveling personal attacks at me for "faking" it.

I suppose it was also inevitable that a portion of the hateful comments would include mockery over the media-fueled fairy-tale marriage. And since it was enough of a struggle to maintain a state of acceptance for this thing we were calling my new normal, I attempted to stay strong without wasting my vital energy in battling them.

I did put up a challenge on social media to any and all internet trolls just before climbing into my hospital bed: anyone who didn't believe me about my injuries or about this amputation could come to the hospital and observe the surgery for themselves. The public had the information now, and there was nothing stopping anyone from showing up and proving this was all "fake."

I mean, given their nasty passion, you would expect them to arrive in droves. You might expect them to have cameras and audio recorders ready to capture every twist in the story.

Not one of the skeptics or deniers showed up.

"Amp Day" was on a Monday. They prepped me, put me under, and finally did the amputation my family and I had struggled to avoid. For me, the time-jump thing happened again, and this time when I woke and looked down at the sheets, the troubled limb was missing, just below the knee. It sounds counterintuitive, but the impact of seeing my truncated leg was not particularly bad.

Maybe I was inoculated from most of the shock because I had spent a lot of time reading up on the procedure. In addition, I was so thoroughly burned out from the struggle that the main thought that went through my head at the sight of my new leg stump was *Finally*.

The leg was gone and there were no surgical complications. As for the rest of my recovery, I could stop trying to roll the boulder up the mountain.

Two days after the operation, I was still in the hospital but my head had cleared after the anesthesia. The pain meds were light enough to allow me to be wide awake, so a bunch of family members and friends were all there to help me welcome phase two of my new normal. It was quite a crowd for that small room: Mom and Dad, my sisters, my fairy-tale husband, and my Boston nurses, Tracy and Naomi.

Even with a group that large, my PTSD was pretty well contained by my comfort with these people. The sense of safety in their presence was a welcome relief to my anxious reactions at any other public gathering.

I lay there in modest hospital attire, chatting away with one family member after another, while I casually opened the mail my husband had brought in from home. Even in the hospital, I handled paying our bills.

So there I was, absently going through one bill after another, when I came to a medium-sized envelope with no return address. I assumed it was just a letter from someone out in the public who knew about my surgery. We had received several positive messages like that in the past.

This handwritten note didn't tell me to get well soon.

The "letter" was accompanied by a printout of someone's text message trail. That someone had my husband's name and contact information. When I ran my eyes down the page, the wording in the texts convinced me they were from him.

The anonymous note openly accused my husband of cheating on our marriage. And it certainly seemed to me that I was holding a printout of his text conversations with his lover.

There are moments, hopefully rare, when we experience such a powerful rush of dread throughout our bodies that it really does feel as if our blood has instantly turned to ice water. That happened to me, while the others in the room continued talking.

But my husband saw the look on my face and realized something was going on. He snatched the printout away, but I was pretty fierce in demanding it back.

I may have been a tad loud. All other conversation stopped. Everyone looked as if another bomb had gone off, this time right there in the room.

I asked for a moment of privacy, and the next thing I knew the room was cleared and it was just the two of us. I looked back at the little care package from the anonymous stranger. What I saw there was a saga of betrayal.

Of course, there was an alternate explanation energetically offered to me. And maybe, if this had been the first inkling that something was wrong, I could have gone into denial over it. But as soon as I saw his words to her, and her replies to him, it was as if the tumblers inside a dozen different locks all clicked into place at the same moment. I was sick inside and speechless. How awful for the family to come to my hospital room for the purpose of celebrating but go away with such a terrible pall over the afternoon.

Naturally, the pall was darkest over the two of us. I emerged from the hospital a couple of days later minus one leg and plus one broken marriage. It would take a few more months to finalize the decision to divorce and try to prepare Noah for the disappointment of it, but that day the vessel cracked wide open. The sense of loss was like falling into an abyss. Worst of all, my heart broke for Noah and for his sense of family. I hated the thought of causing him to feel abandoned.

The sense of failure felt as heavy as an iron suit. We tried couple's counseling, but it failed. The kindly Edd Hendee even took him to lunch to talk things over, but when they were done, Mr. Hendee let me know that in his opinion, sadly, my marriage was over. What he thought meant a lot to me. He was the person who married us and also walked us through premarital counseling. If anyone wanted us to succeed, it was him.

———

I hung on to what I wished was the truth, against my own better judgment, until New Year's Eve, which was the day I was finally scheduled to take my first trial steps on the new artificial leg. Yes, it would be only the first of countless more steps, but this was a major turning point in my new normal. I knew my attitude would greatly affect how well it worked for me.

I needed that moment to feel like my first baby steps in returning to upright motion again, and this could happen only if every point of physical discomfort or awkwardness that came from the experience was filed in my mind as merely being the way it felt to start walking again. If depression or negative thinking invaded the process, those same sensations could come in as symptoms of my loss and limitations, harbingers of all the limitations yet to come.

The greatest challenge wasn't the artificial leg but rather what existed right behind my eyeballs. The old saying "It is what it is" would have to be modified for this, to be more like, "It is how you insist on seeing it." We certainly can't always control our lives, but we can control how we meet challenges. I needed a partner in that hour to help me settle the way this thing was going to look and feel for the foreseeable future. He had social plans, though.

This was when I knew I had to bite the bullet and tell Noah what was going on. Knowing the marriage was broken was not enough. Now my mom's experience in her broken marriage became the experience base for my own. Like her, I had to do something.

For me, much of the experience of the word *handicap* lies in the way I see it and interpret it. The only handicap is in aspects of loss we have no way to remedy. So I avoided fixating on things that appeared impossible, for now, and found that this selective form of vision was essential to maintaining concentration and focusing on difficult goals.

When the larger picture loomed up and felt overwhelming, as it certainly did, my only answer was to get more focused. *Do this. . . . Now do this. . . . Now do this. . . .* like a brick mason using blocks the size of sugar cubes to build a cathedral.

That brick mason surely knows one great truth about the task ahead: don't look up, or the view will dismay you with the challenge it represents. Instead, pick up one block, move it into place, set it down, and then pick up the next block.

No matter how small my gain on the overall architectural plan might appear, there was calming comfort in the routine itself, and comfort as well in each row of well-laid bricks. I set to work.

As gently as I could, I sat Noah down and began to explain to my little boy that this marriage was in trouble. I told him it made me very sad to say this, but it would soon be just the two of us again. Noah floored me when he took my news right in stride and just responded, "Okay." No emotion, no questions about what was going on. I was more than a little surprised by his calm demeanor, since he can raise his share of boyish drama. I asked him about it.

Noah then told me a story of seeing my husband communicating on Facetime with a female. The way they were talking caused Noah to believe she was his girlfriend. He was old enough that it bothered him to see it, but he kept quiet because he had no idea how to approach me with what he saw. Without my knowledge, he had already sweated it out alone. He had been hoping it would just go away, because the idea of bringing it to me was overwhelming. It made him feel like he was helping to beat up his mom.

"It's okay, Mom," Noah told me. "He shouldn't have been doing that." He seemed genuinely relieved. It was just one more reminder to me that smart kids are often far more observant than we know. I made a mental note: *Just because he can ignore me doesn't mean he isn't hearing me. All the time.*

I also made myself a firm promise that I would never again bring home a man who wasn't someone my son could emotionally trust. I would never put him in the position where he felt he had to keep a toxic secret just to maintain peace in the house.

Of course, it's so easy to make a statement like that. And although I can now look back knowing I have been able to keep it, the gritty truth is that dealing with deception is a fundamental part of life in this world. I can't promise Noah or anyone else that I will never be deceived again. We all know that liars lie and the good ones can get you to swear to it.

I'm not trying to paint rainbows over a landfill. There's no reason to pretend that the haters failed to notice the breakup of my fairy-tale marriage—in a big way.

No one doubts that the opportunity to project anonymous online hatred offers an addictive rush of power to those who are tormented by frustration in their real lives. The bad news for them is that the rush is short and the need runs deep. The bad news for everyone else is that this means the haters are always hard at work getting a new fix.

I didn't need public shaming anyway. I had plenty of my own. The humiliation over losing this marriage was paralyzing. It had a deeper and more painful effect on me than the amputation itself. I hated hearing my father's voice, broadcasting from a point about two inches behind my eyes and repeating on a loop, *What a dope you are! Are you going to mess up everything you do, all your life? What a dope . . .*

I was lost and my life felt out of control. I was thankful for my parents and their loving generosity, but at the same time, my son needed his mom off of the injured list, and I had been thrown, to say the least.

My prayers got back nothing that felt like an answer.

This doesn't mean no answer came. But when it did, the form it took was something new to me. The best way for me to describe it for you is that the distinct feeling of being guided forward, one step at a time, came over me. It went on, step after quiet step. Nothing was solved for me, but I was strengthened and supported to find the solution myself.

*Part Five*

# RUNNING
# TOWARD
# A *New*
# NORMAL

# -14-

# Looking for the Helpers

While I was still recovering from the amputation, FBI agents visited me again. (I don't have many problems with boredom.) They were getting ready to begin prosecuting their case and wanted to advise me that I could expect to be subpoenaed to testify.

I felt as if they had just leaned over my bed and stabbed me. The thought of facing that murdering coward again was revolting.

What could I do? Ever since I had caught sight of his face on one of the early newscasts, I had seen him and his older brother again and again in nightmares. It was like dreaming of running from a train when you can't jump off the tracks; I could never escape them when they haunted me. I could never find my little boy in those terrible dreams. I never knew if I should chase them and find out what they had done with him or run from them and perhaps live long enough to help him in another way.

To hide, to attack them, to run away screaming—none of it ever did any good. I hated the helplessness of the nightmares they had left me with as much as I reviled the helplessness of lying out in that street with my body shot full of shrapnel and my little boy injured and terrified.

Now the FBI wanted me to breathe the same air as this monster. I stiffened my back and got ready for a battle of wills with the government.

Did you know FBI interviewers are very clever? Instead of getting tough about everything, which I must admit would have hardened my stance, they quietly explained the importance of offering some measure of justice to the dead and wounded. They very respectfully spoke to me about the number of loved ones they had to interview over this tragedy, all feeling the impact of those bombs.

They didn't need to remind me that there was already little enough anyone could do. By that point I had lived through many months of bedridden time, when I was free to think things over. I had read the investigative findings about the bombers and their methods, the interviews with other survivors, the testimonies of loved ones. I had a much clearer picture than I wanted to have of the misery inflicted by those two killers. I also had a strong sense that it was somehow my duty to understand as much as I could about this thing. And since I knew what I knew, the FBI agents didn't have to work that hard to convince me.

It was unthinkable that this man's lawyers might find a loophole to slip him through. There was no way to know if my testimony would prove key to securing a conviction, but if my presence could help in any way, I had to be there.

The clever agents quite accurately judged me to be someone who could never live with seeing the surviving bomber either walk free or take a low-level slap on the wrist as his sentence. The thought that I could be even partially responsible for something like that would be devastating.

Sometimes you can only shake your head. I agreed to testify and to do the best I could. Nobody said I had to like it.

When people ask me how I could psyche up the courage to begin preparing to go to court, I give the credit to the late Fred Rogers of the old TV show *Mister Rogers' Neighborhood*. His program ran for so many years because of his gentle tone of wisdom. I never forgot his words when he quoted his mother's advice about coping with disaster and the disillusionment that can follow it. He said she told him to "look for the helpers." There will always be helpers.

I surely lived through the truth of that. It was only the brave hearts and strong humanity of those first responders that got me and my little boy off of that street alive. They represented the best of humanity, and I can never forget them.

Online, I was grateful for a powerful outpouring of support from all around the world. Here is a small sample of these wonderful messages, and I can attest that these little electronic bubbles of loving energy, thoughts, and wishes did a world of good. They served as personal floatation devices for my morale and no doubt did the same for every attack victim who got such kind support.

Wish there were more people in the world like you. You are truly inspiring and proof that people can be strong and overcome anything. . . . And one more thing, don't let anyone get to you that is negative about your leg. . . . Just remember you have the coolest leg on the planet!

You truly are a warrior and an inspiration to everyone.

I just wanted to write and let you know that I think you are such an amazing strong person. I have been following your page and it's very inspiring.

I wanted to say thank you for your inspiring attitude, drive, and determination. Also the humor! (It's not you, it's me.)

I've found myself in a rough patch lately but your words of hope and encouragement (and I read a lot of them!) have lifted my spirits and given me this excitement for tomorrow! You are an inspiration and God knows every time you post something, or let everyone know you're having a "human" day too, or share the brilliant things in life you see, you're opening someone's eyes to the way life *should* be seen.

When I read what you post, I have hope. I know I am a survivor and not a victim anymore. . . . God bless you and know you are in my prayers. Nothing will hold you back!

I admire you not because your life is perfect but because your life is a mess and you still find the beauty in every day.

Thank you for being the biggest hero to someone you don't even know.

I haven't worn shorts in thirty years and today I saw your post, with you in a dress exposing your fake leg and scars. I decided I could do it too.

If I had tendered any doubts about going through with my trial testimony, these people and so many kind others made those doubts vanish. I could hardly honor those helpers who had swarmed out onto that Boston street in the wake of the explosions unless I took my own opportunity to be a helper as well.

Anytime I felt my determination falter, all I had to do was picture the pattern of blast injuries across my legs and back, remembering that this same pattern would have been across my little boy's back and head, with his head at the exact level where the worst blast damage was done to my legs. That was all it took to restore my determination.

Without an overwhelming guilty verdict and strong sentencing, there could never be a guarantee that someone else's child wouldn't be hit with terrible explosions one day as a direct result of this man's miserable handiwork. Nobody had to convince me that he had forfeited his right to ever walk free among us again.

For this reason, I had no choice but to live out the example I wanted to set for my little boy and to be consistent with the expectations I placed upon him. In spite of all the wonderful help and support that had blessed me since the bombs went off, this was something I had to take care of myself. It was time to jump on Mr. Rogers's bandwagon and not just look for the helpers but join them.

There was little formal pretrial preparation for me beyond a couple of interviews, since I was only going to speak about my small slice of that afternoon. Nobody had to freshen my memory of it.

In fact, the persistence of those memories was a big part of my PTSD battle and my constant struggle to beat back the resulting anxiety. I could understand how a soldier re-turning from combat can find himself or herself flat on the floor because a car just backfired outside. If a trash truck drops a dumpster on the street, a frozen rush goes straight up my spine. And you can probably imagine why I won't be attending any fireworks displays, yes? The gut-thud of the largest fireworks would only duplicate my memory of the shock wave. Some people who were close to the finish line but not present at the detonations thought that the explo-sions actually were fireworks. The hairs on the back of my neck probably don't know the difference between the sounds.

So for the coming trial, my main task was just to embrace the fact that I was going to face this man down in a court of law. If I could focus on the potential positives, this terrible encounter with a true-life monster might actually be an op-portunity. The testimony was a fact, but how it would affect me was a matter of my own choosing.

This was another one of those situations that becomes whatever you say it is, as long as you say it with enough conviction and don't waver under pressure. This is how I was able to shape that piece of reality like a handful of clay and move from fear to determination.

# -15-

# Serious Improvements to the New Normal

After that milestone, my day-to-day life began to move in a positive direction in things unrelated to athletics. The first inklings of an answer began to form as to how I was going to best use this new lease on life.

I had no idea there were people whose job is to find potential public speakers and represent them. But people at the Premiere Speakers Bureau had seen me in the media and wanted to give me an opportunity to try public speaking. They called with an offer to represent me, provided I was willing to pursue public speaking in a serious way. They explained that they understood the importance of my faith and assured me they would try to book me in places where people wanted to hear a story like mine. Was I interested?

Now, there was no rainbow that suddenly threw an arch over me. Nobody played an ascending glissando on the harp, and there was no one singing "Yahhh!" in musical exclamation. It only felt that way.

There was just me, mouth moving like a silent fish while I tried to find my voice and throw out a hearty acceptance of the idea. I was a nervous speaker who battled stage fright, but the speakers bureau was offering me a chance to use that terrible event as an opportunity to address so many people I would otherwise never reach. This felt like a second chance at life, to do things better than the first time around.

Many of the people I have come to meet through these speaking engagements are my brothers and sisters in Christ. Others are people who don't share the Christian faith but who are sincere in their drive to live their lives on positive terms. I welcome friendly exchanges with all of them, because we strengthen one another's resolve to remain true to our callings and I believe God uses our longings to draw us to himself.

I don't have to know the million tiny connections that will fit together to make that happen in each person's life. Instead I observe that the perseverance, sincerity, spiritual longing, and rise of compassion and empathy will all combine to ultimately lead to a surprise encounter with God, who is as close to us as the sensation of drawing a breath.

---

When that first phone call with the speakers bureau ended, my insecurities kicked in. I wondered if my ambition to speak would fall flat. Did I want to deal with more media attention? Could I take my thoughts and feelings and form them into the right words, well enough to ask strangers to embrace them? I felt the appeal of the idea but I also felt startled and overwhelmed. All I could do was start writing down words from my heart, which wasn't hard because writing was how I chose to express myself even as a little girl.

The very next day the speakers bureau called with my first booking. Within a week, they had me booked for the rest of the year.

Okay, wow. Nothing normal about that. Turns out there is a large audience out there who will not ask me to leave out my faith in telling my story. Some are secular audiences, while others can appreciate my spiritual journey for what it is. I wonder if this audience exists because, in the midst of pain and tragedy, we are all hungry for contact with others who live in Christ. We know the recharging that goes along with genuine fellowship, the feeling of the presence of God's power that comes most strongly in community.

I got a powerful sensation from this opportunity, that of being picked up and swept along. Suddenly, everything was moving fast, just as it had with the fairy-tale wedding. Only this time I resolved to keep my hands firmly on the controls. These first few small speaking engagements were supposed to be my cautious attempt to test the waters with my story. Now it was more than that. It felt like someone lit a rocket engine under me.

I was determined to be deliberate in how I proceeded. My story was more universal than I realized. That meant it was worth slowing things down and doing it right. The number of speaking requests I received revealed a hunger to look at life through a spiritual lens, one that allows us to see the seemingly endless line of disasters and tragedies in the news as being first and foremost challenges to our spirits and to our hearts. We face these challenges best with the simple tools of prayer, dedicated action, and fellowship. They may not change the landscape, but they help us adapt to the terrain.

I spoke in the town of Steubenville, Ohio, and afterward people came by to say hello. A number of them were moved to tears and talked of personally relating to my story of fighting to take my life back, partly from the Boston Marathon killers but also from the internal voices of judgment and limitation that plagued parts of my life.

After this particular event, a boy of about ten walked up with his father. He smiled at me and said, "I have to tell you that you're my hero."

My reply was brilliant. I gulped and said, "Really?"

"Oh, yeah. I only came today with my dad, you know, because he wanted to come. But you changed how I see things." He proceeded to hand me a handwritten note that he had prepared in case we didn't get to speak, which told me again how much the event meant to him.

This wonderful experience of positive feedback has been repeated in many other places. It never gets old, and it's one of the best feelings I've ever known.

And I have still never found anything more healing than helping someone else. I'm not sure how it works, but just doing it seems to feed my life with invisible vitamins. Things just get better.

———

The amputation of my left leg was performed on November 10, 2014. Of course, we also had that other explosion two days later with the envelope at the hospital room party, then it was off to rehab and back home.

I was hungry to pump some physical strength into my muscles and bones after so many months of immobility. So two weeks after the amputation, as soon as I was discharged from the rehabilitation center, I went back to my old gym and began to work out again, trying to recapture a little of that old feeling of being strong, of feeling capable. I craved it.

But remember I was only at the Boston Marathon as an observer. Everybody crossing the finish line that day was in better condition than I was. A few years earlier I had tried to run a minimarathon, and even on two good legs it was an ordeal. I had decided that I would never fall in love with the sport and concluded I would most likely never be a runner unless someone was chasing me. I told myself that I burned enough calories on nervous energy to replace a daily run of three miles.

Now I started going in for workouts six days a week, and the gym kindly referred me to a personal trainer. He was a young man who was also a single leg amputee, below the knee. He had lost his leg in a motorcycle accident a few years earlier, and since then he had physically rehabilitated himself and mastered the use of his prosthetic leg. I'm sure you've already guessed that I signed up to work with him on the spot.

He proved to be a strong and consistent taskmaster who embraced my goal of regaining my strength. Here's a sample of his mindset, and the mindset he encouraged in me. The day after receiving my prosthetic leg, I returned to the gym and began wearing it to workouts. But the stump end of my leg was getting rubbed raw, so I heeded my doctors' warnings not to overuse the prosthesis and the next day decided to go to the gym with my crutches instead of using the prosthesis.

My trainer took one look at me and asked what was wrong. So I told him I was tired of the soreness of using the leg and I wanted a break for the day.

Oops.

He gently but firmly insisted that I must *never* come to the gym with crutches. I had to promise to get rid of them. "We aren't just working out the rest of your body except for the missing leg. We're working out the entire body's ability to use that leg in the most organic and natural manner that we can. You can't achieve that by worrying about skin irritation, because you can't achieve that without the leg."

Harsh, yes? Maybe harsh is just what I needed, because as much as I wanted to remain positive in my recovery, the lifelong task of living with this thing felt like looking up at Mt. Everest from the base.

The truth in his words was plain, and I couldn't see any way forward except to embrace it. From then on, I did the workouts with the fake leg and without the crutches. Part of my new normal was this: from now on, unless I was wearing that leg, I would never be fully dressed.

My main workout was structured around heavy core work. General aerobic exercises of all sorts were added to fire up the process of regaining vital strength for my heart and lungs. Since my blood pressure was always lower than normal because of the remaining effects of POTS from my teen years, I focused on raising it with the physical effort of the workouts.

At home, I struggled with the aftermath of pulling apart this little family. That situation guaranteed that I had plenty of stress energy to work out at the gym.

When New Year's Eve rolled around and I took my first steps in the new artificial leg alone, I firmly acknowledged not only that the marriage was no longer a part of my life but also that my fake leg was now a permanent part of it. I accepted these two truths, but they gave me the distinct sensation of falling into a hole and dropping at high speed.

As for the new leg, I took my first walking steps between a pair of handrails, for stability.

The physical feeling of standing up was good, but I could instantly tell that this was going to be radically different from the way I remembered standing. *Here you are*, I told myself, working on my confidence on New Year's Day. *You are more or less upright, without using crutches, for the first time since April 15, 2013. The view from here, standing up fully straight and without hunching over crutches, back straight and eyes forward, is a familiar view from the old normal. You remember this.*

I had two legs beneath me now, but I could only feel the ground with one of them. The sensation reminded me of times when I still had two good legs but had slept in a funny position so that one leg fell asleep. We all know that sensation of standing up on a leg so numb that you can't feel it. Now I had the same sensation, only this time the missing leg was no illusion. When I stood up on the prosthesis, the leg clearly didn't belong to me. It really made it hard to find my balance.

It was immediately apparent that I would need intense practice to develop the necessary skill. And good balance and smooth movement would require strong support from every one of the muscles I was working to build up at the gym.

When I considered the challenge, it felt like something I could learn to do but only after serious practice. It would take a lot of hard work before I would be able to move with sure steps on this new leg and carry myself with any sort of grace.

163

I embraced the task. But while I went through that first process of walking between the parallel bars, ready to grab them if I needed to, this new challenge of learning to operate a foreign object as if it was a part of my body felt like the idea of learning how to ride a unicycle.

By that I mean most people could learn to ride a unicycle if they had a strong enough reason to endure the process of finding their balance on it. Why, they could bring their unicycle into my physical therapy lab and share time on these same parallel bars, just as I was doing on the leg.

And the strong and positive side of human nature pretty much guarantees that somewhere out there is a determined someone who also stands on an artificial limb (or two) and has now mastered walking and running—and will next learn to ride that unicycle, and maybe juggle while doing it.

I understand that level of striving. It's buried in the nature that drives us, is it not? Even as we lament the terrible dark sides of humanity that can sweep over us from time to time, it's glorious to consider the great accomplishments that our same human nature can achieve.

---

I went through a brief period of rehab at my doctor's office, building up the amount of time my stump could tolerate the stresses of the prosthesis. I was told I would not be pronounced fit to continue on my own until I could run the length of the doctor's office hallway, up and back. I started with a few steps at a time in each direction.

So since my new leg and I would be spending so much time together, I decided she ought to have a name and dubbed her Felicia. Together, Felicia and I began our new tradition of matching pedicures. Then I put my newly emerging core muscle strength to work on lifting and supporting the motion of my fake leg, employing muscles to walk and move in ways I never used before.

Today's prostheses are impressive, but they are still not like the real thing. This means all of the other muscles involved in walking and in balance need to make up the difference. Stomach and side lifts, back raises, side step running—we did it all, and also what felt like every other motion the core muscles of the human torso could be put through.

When the day came that I was able to run up and down the doctor's office hallway with a measure of confidence and stability, the rehabilitation officially ended. After that, it was my trainer and me at the gym. This man became such a powerful influence on my physical recovery that the whole workout program and its screaming difficulty did more than whip me into condition. It lifted my morale around the clock.

We all know the worst thing about life-changing decisions is the anticipation of all the risks. Once the decision is made and we can begin dealing with putting things back together, things may still be difficult but our worst fears usually sink back into the depths and we can cope after that. I began to feel that effect kick in.

Outside of the training sessions, once I had named my prosthetic leg Felicia and saw to it that her pedicure matched my other foot, I began to build up the amount of time I could tolerate the friction of the prosthesis against what remained of my leg. In spite of the difficulties, my spirits were good because it was such a relief to have independent motion again, even if only for a couple of hours at a time.

Noah loved seeing me fully upright again. I'm certain he saw how much it meant to me. He tuned right in to that and danced around radiating joy for both of us. Noah still likes to refer to me as his "robot mom."

With each new smile Noah and I exchange, both of us understand that we are only present together in this life because the worst shrapnel somehow missed us. And we will never for one second take that for granted.

My trainer pushed me like a pile driver, just relentless, while never failing to make me feel supported. He had full compassion and respect for what Noah and I had gone through with the terrorist attacks, but as far as this business of living with one leg and a prosthesis was concerned, he didn't want to hear a lot of whining. As a result, once my muscle fibers got through the shock of his workout attack, they began to tighten and build in response. With every workout I felt the strengthening process going on, and it was wonderful.

How wonderful? We've all seen the shots of those gasping climbers who have just reached the peak of some great mountain. There they are, arms in the air, elated. The photo pulls us in; we can almost feel the freezing air they are breathing. Their victory is real, whether they survive the trip back down the mountain or not. They have pressed through every obstacle and risk and arrived to plant their flag.

Oh, I felt all that. No exaggeration. After spending all those months in bed and taking thirty-seven different drugs for pain and infection, after weeks spent with my leg held above the level of my heart to keep a shift in blood pressure off the leg sutures, here we were.

The process of getting in shape was a painful luxury. But when I made the final decision to amputate, I also made myself a promise that I would never let my disability define my ambitions. Even though I had only attended the 2013 Boston Marathon as a spectator, and in spite of my nonathletic past, I made a goal to return to Boston to run, and this became an important part of my new normal, a message to send myself. This was no time for a pity party; it was time to define myself as successful and recovered.

So on top of getting myself back in shape for life out of bed and on my feet, I began training to run the next Boston Marathon. I was supposed to wear the new prosthesis for only about an hour at a time until my leg adjusted to it. Right or wrong, I skipped that part. For weeks, after my gym workouts, I would hang out at the mall and watch people walk, making myself copy their movements. I forced myself to take steps as if both my legs were still there instead of shifting my weight to the side with each step and taking stress off the amputated leg. I ignored the pain and focused on walking with a natural gait.

Three months after the amputation, the limb was still painful and sore but I began jogging in short bursts around the gym and on the basketball court. I went through regimens of hop-and-skip exercises like those a football player or a boxer might use to gain strength, balance, and speed.

The resulting swelling at the amputation site kept me going to the prosthetist's office once or twice each week so they could adjust the fit to minimize my pain enough to keep me moving.

My first one-mile test run was a killer. But I practiced tuning out the discomfort and kept increasing the distance day by day. Two weeks before the marathon, I managed a sixteen-mile day! Oh, it was glorious to feel all that ground, all that distance, churning away beneath my feet. The memory of every day spent in a prone position or lying on my side trying to find a position that hurt a little less drove me to push for greater distance. The helpless feeling of lying with my leg elevated, luxuriating in my five minutes of Dangle Time, was still strong in my mind. I loved the way that every single footstep seemed to strike back at that helpless feeling.

I had no need to lose weight and I mostly like to eat healthy food anyway, so I didn't really change my diet for the training. I did make an effort to be more disciplined about my food intake, but I confess I failed. Chocolate chip cookies have always been my weakness.

My old problem with asthma returned, aggravated by all the gasping and panting. It was clear that I was starting from scratch after a year and a half in bed. I would exercise for one or two hours, then do another set of exercises at home in the evenings. The moves had to be adjusted to the prosthesis. For example, I can't bend as much as before, since Felicia doesn't respond as a real leg would. Balance is a constant challenge. In doing squats, the angles of my leg and foot have to be exact. To run, I have to think of *how* to place my leg on every step a millisecond before landing.

Marathoners talk about "hitting the wall," referring to a point of exhaustion that makes a runner feel so empty it can stop them as surely as running into a brick wall. I hit the wall on that sixteen-mile day, but it wasn't me; it was my artificial leg.

I was running on a prosthesis called a blade. It takes the pounding of the runner's steps better because it uses its springy quality to propel you forward instead of using an ankle joint, which can be prone to failure from running long distances.

But even the cushioned impacts of running on the ankleless blade failed to protect my leg stump from the beating I was giving it, and on that sixteen-mile day my suture scars broke open inside the socket of the leg. This was a major setback. Running a marathon in that condition was out.

With only fourteen days left to go, there was no way to recover in time to make the whole run. Still, I felt that there were people who needed to see me do this, and I needed it for myself as well. Since it had been about 3.2 months since I had gotten the prosthesis, I picked a distance of 3.2 miles and asked the race officials if I could be allowed to run those final miles of the race. People have tried to jump into the final miles of the race before and risked being caught and disgraced. But the officials very kindly said it would be okay for me to do that.

So my trainer became Super Trainer by deciding to go to Boston and run alongside me, to be sure my morale stayed high and my determination did not falter. You see how lucky I was to have found a trainer like this, don't you? What a gift to be on the receiving end of such kind support.

—

So we did it, and on race day, at 3.2 miles from the finish line, we stepped into the flowing crowd and began to run. By that point I already knew from experience that there is terrible pain and there is good pain. Every athlete knows what I mean when I say "good pain," and it's certainly not that the pain is a pleasant experience. It means that the pain is at a level you can tolerate and hurts less because you bring it on yourself out of choice. You know the pain represents the long-term benefit of working out and growing stronger, of building endurance.

I was running on a partial leg that should have had a lot more healing time before I set out to do this. It was hard but the pain was acceptable under the circumstances. My mom and dad, my sister Allie, my nurses Tracy and Naomi, and a whole group of wonderfully supportive friends, were at the finish line to see if I could make it. I couldn't let them down. It isn't that I thought anyone would be upset with me if I failed; it was that I knew their loving-kindness was such that it would be painful for them if I collapsed, because their hearts were with me.

But as I got close to the finish line I began to falter. The pain in my leg had built up steadily from the time we'd started out, and it felt as if I had gravel in the socket of the prosthetic leg that was grinding into me with every step. Once the pain reached that level, it quickly escalated. Soon the entire socket of the prosthesis felt as if it were lined with grit that was cutting away at my flesh.

Everything disintegrated quickly after that. Even with the finish line in view, I became seriously concerned that I just wouldn't be able to get that far. The fresh wound on my leg began to send out those same sensations of burning that I recalled so well from the day of the attacks.

Now the finish line was only a hundred yards or so in the distance, and every step felt like a stab in the leg with an ice pick. I had worked so hard to walk and run without a limp, but now I was rolling to the side with every step as my body instinctively tried to ease the pain of each foot strike.

The fear hit me then. It looked as if I was going to go down only a few yards from the finish line. My body was objecting to every move I made.

It was bad enough to be unable to go the full distance, but the effect of failing even this truncated run would be devastating to my self-esteem. After all, I had announced publicly that I could complete this run, and to fail would call into question my strength and determination, something I could not imagine doing. No matter what the future might hold for me, I never had any doubt that without a clear sense of my own strength and a belief in my power of determination, I risked moving from being handicapped to being an invalid.

*Invalid* is quite a word, isn't it? It's one of those words that makes me glad our population has become so much more sensitive about language and its effect on people. To be invalid, by implication, is to fail to be valid, and to not be valid is to be less than others. But this is a condition of the mind, not the body.

That dire condition starts at the moment we accept the cruel or thoughtless things people say to us. As a strong woman, I could brush off the random cruelties of daily living, but if I allowed myself to become an invalid in my mind, those insults would land on fertile ground. The disintegration of my self-concept would begin. I would become a cripple.

I kept running.

I approached the finish line with a pronounced limp. It took everything I had to keep my left leg from buckling and dropping me to the pavement.

My leg was fully on fire, but the end was so close that as long as I could make it move another step, I could not give up.

I don't even know where I got those last few hundred strides from, but I was certainly at the end of my rope.

I fell as soon as I crossed the finish line and felt as though I didn't have a single stride left in me.

---

It was only a 3.2 mile run, far less than what so many others endured out there. But I felt a kindred spirit with those ultramarathoners who torture their bodies on hundred-mile runs through the desert. I'd reached the end in spite of all the difficulties, and the most important statement I made that day I made to myself. My purpose was to negate the disability that had been inflicted on me in a symbolic way.

A woman named Alyssa got it, in spades. She found the group of nurses and family who waited for me at the finish line, and waited with them for hours just to see me cross it, and she was soaking wet and crying when I saw her. We just stood and hugged for the longest time.

Not long after the race, she left her photo on my Facebook wall, along with a message:

Rebekah, I know you don't know me very well . . . [but if] April 15, 2013, changed your life in ways you could have never imagined, it also changed mine. I was going through a rough patch in life, nothing at all compared to what you and so many others faced that day. . . . You and all the other survivors touched me in ways I will never be able to express in words. . . . So to see you cross that finish line, Rebekah [two years after the 2013 Marathon], it was completely and utterly overwhelming. . . . I will forever think of you whenever I need to cross little finish lines of my own.

This was a solid milestone for me and another reminder that my process of recovery and my way of trying to live a meaningful life were actually combining to make small but positive differences in the world.

———

In Alabama a short time later, I was taking some time to meet people and take photos with them before speaking after dinner later that evening. A young woman approached me and earnestly told me she wanted to thank me for working to inspire people and that her mother was a new amputee who had just lost one of her legs as well. Unlike me, her mom was avoiding the use of an artificial leg, leaving her stuck in a wheelchair. She felt too self-conscious about her condition to leave the house much. But her daughter wanted to assure me that her mom would have come to see me that night if she could.

You know how something can hit you so hard and so deep in your heart that it feels like you instantly gain about twenty or thirty pounds? Your flesh hangs heavy on your bones. Your energy supply dips. You realize that you're way behind on your sitting down.

That's how it felt when I imagined allowing this woman to miss out, if this was where she wanted to be. So much of the trouble in her life was beyond my reach, but this one thing was something I could change for the better. I felt my heart speed up a little.

I asked her how quickly she could get home, and she said it would take only ten minutes. This meant that ten minutes away a woman was struggling with finding her new normal just as I had struggled, and was still struggling, to find my own, battling inevitable depression over the loss of her old normal. I had no trouble imagining the social anxiety that kept this woman alone. I didn't have to be told that she only hid at home because she felt lost.

When I tried to imagine how my behavior and my attitude would have been affected if I had to go through my surgeries and long recovery without my support network, the heavy feeling got worse. This girl's mother had suffered her accident and amputation only to return home to the task of mothering her daughter while recovering in the house alone. She was a living example of what I had been spared by the love of my family.

So I asked this young woman to go back home and invite her mother to be my personal guest that evening, and in the meantime, I stayed and had a word with the organizers. It's great to have a sold-out audience, but we all know there are always two more spots to be found.

When the daughter returned with her reluctant mom for the evening's event, the organizers squeezed in two more seats at a table for them. We had the chance to talk after dinner and, of course, both wound up in tears. I completely empathized with her feeling of being shamed by her new limitations. I gently but emphatically insisted that there can't be any shame in random disasters, only in our reactions to them.

I also insisted that her brave act that day in leaving the house and coming to see me, ignoring the urge to feel self-conscious and instead embracing action, was a perfect model for her best response to this new normal of hers. I told her truthfully about my own struggles to define my new normal and to avoid having it defined for me by physical limitation.

I let her know that I have to constantly seek ways to work around everything that was taken from me that day.

Beyond that, I asked her to begin pushing herself to get out of the house, even for routine chores. And as for the future . . . I extended my prosthetic leg and introduced her to Felicia.

The leg looks like the mechanical device that it is, with a normal-looking foot attached. I explained my practice of always keeping Felicia's toenails painted to match my real ones, and it doesn't make any difference to me that the leg is obviously fake. I want matching toenails, no apologies.

As for the fact that I have rejected the use of a cosmetic artificial leg, even though they can make ones now that look almost like the real thing, I don't like the idea of hiding my condition. To me, wearing the mechanical leg has a nice feeling of honesty.

She got it. I actually saw the idea take hold with her. And I know she took it home and put it into play, in terms of what would work for her. I didn't give her the will to act; I only pointed out a possible route. She was willing to dare to trust me because I could assure her from personal experience that this route could take her to a much more fulfilling and joyful experience of being alive.

After all, she had already shown the desire to break out of her self-imposed jail cell by accepting my invitation and showing up with her daughter. All she needed, I was convinced, was a framework to hang the idea of succeeding on.

My personal choice is to use audacity to confront fear. By audacity I don't mean recklessness, such as starting kicking fights with two-legged people. Rather, I mean wearing a mechanical artificial leg with shorts and sandals (and matching nail polish, naturally) while out shopping on a warm summer day. Or any other day.

This visit taught me something about my own strength. In my worst moments of fear and insecurity, I can know that I am strong enough to help someone else. My fears might be real, but so is my strength.

I'm certain the clincher for this woman was when I told her that this new normal of hers, of life as an amputee, isn't a noble Hollywood story with a happy ending. There is no sunset to ride off into, just more life. There will be dark days when discouragement seems to ooze from the walls, dismaying confrontations with inconsiderate people occur, and reminders are everywhere that the old normal is gone, along with the capabilities she once knew. But if she could find it within herself to allow her audacity to come out and get some fresh air, then all that time spent outside the house would allow independent experiences and opportunities to pile up. Getting outside the security of home would become easier with repetition. It was time for her to go back to mixing it up with life on the come-and-get-me level.

And since I knew this was the truth of my own life, I could speak confidently to her. I'm certain we both went home stronger.

—

I consider myself fortunate to be able to travel. I can appreciate the irony of the fact that, if not for the bombing, I wouldn't be meeting these people and hearing their stories. All that fellowship would have been lost. It isn't an even trade, but it's a testimony of God's grace in the aftermath.

It's not all sunshine and roses. My tap dancing career was extinguished even before it started, but I get to meet some wonderful people I would otherwise never have encountered.

On days when things go well, I get to connect with another soul. These moments are gifts I am always grateful to accept. We both walk away stronger.

One day I was walking through an airport and, as always, the artificial leg was beginning to grate on my skin after hours of use. I can tell you that those long airport corridors or endless walkways in front of the terminals are not friendly to amputees. Although I had become much better at using the leg, after a maximum of two hours the socket would start to feel like it was lined with rocks and pressure pains would begin to spark with hot stabs throughout my left side.

So you can understand how my spirit might tend to flag during the tedium of an airport hike. It isn't a big deal, and it isn't enough to make me forget how close I came to not being around at all or that others were hit worse, with double amputations and giant doses of shrapnel throughout their bodies.

Nevertheless, a sore place on the skin can be a persistent source of torment when all the pressure of standing up is transferred to a small point on the artificial leg. On this day at the airport, I was feeling exhausted and ready to get the thing off and sit down.

But that's when I was waved down by a male amputee who happened to be about my age. I suppose any amputee can spot another at a distance. He also recognized my face from media stories and called me by name. He wanted to let me know that he had lost his leg several years before, and he'd had time to adjust to his prosthesis.

He had even run the 2014 Boston Marathon on his prosthetic leg in honor of all those who had lost life and limb to those two terrorists. On this day, all he wanted to do was greet me, shake hands, and tell me he was inspired by my spiritual message. He also assured me that the feel of my artificial leg would grow more natural over time, as it had with him.

In that moment, with the stump of my leg throbbing away, this was wonderful news to hear. So it turned out we each had affirmation to offer the other, even in such a brief encounter. I got to see the power of faith at work in the life of someone I would otherwise never meet, with whom I would have no connection, and he got to see the effect his reassurance had on me.

This new normal has shown itself to have an unlimited capacity to be harsh and cold but it also has its moments of joy, beautiful little surprises that pop up even on a routine day.

The challenges that arrived with my new normal and remain with me today can seem endless, but the feeling of joy remains the same.

# -16-

# The Terrorists' Leftovers

For the first couple months of 2015, my life was filled by time at home and time on the road for speaking events. I was especially glad for my busy schedule because it was a handy distraction that allowed me to keep my head up and my spirits high. The trial date for the surviving Boston bomber was just around the corner.

Noah didn't like the news that I was going back to Boston with my mom and without him. But at age seven he was perfectly able to understand the issue of justice along with the fact that his mother had to go help out with it. I explained to him that it had to be done in order to make certain the man who had done this to us could never do it again to anyone else. You can bet he understood.

The prosecutor's office flew my mother and me to Boston a day before the trial to give me some time to acclimate. They were as thoughtful and supportive as they could be. They even arranged for me to go into the empty courtroom before the trial began so I could see what I would walk into when the bailiff called my name.

The first thing that struck me was that the entire space was smaller than I pictured. Then they showed me where everyone would be seated. The witness stand where I would be giving my testimony was only a few feet from the defendant's chair.

I blanched at the thought of being so close to him and having to testify with his gaze on me. The prosecutor kindly offered to move the witness stand farther away. I agreed with several other witnesses in our group who also wanted it moved.

By that point I had done all the preliminary work in my mind to visualize successfully going through this. I clearly pictured myself helping the prosecutors, testifying without faltering or allowing emotion to choke me, and then returning home in the knowledge that I had been strong. (Spoiler alert: not that easy.)

I wish I could say I struck some sort of brave pose as I went through the bomber's trial in federal court, but from the time the day of my testimony began, I felt like a giant fist had its fingers around me and was slowly tightening its grip throughout the morning. The police brought us to the courthouse from the hotel at around nine a.m., and media vans were all over the place.

The reporters were congregated like a murder of crows. I knew the story had powerful national and international implications, but it was hard to have to run the gauntlet through all of those heated and competitive journalists on top of everything else. Their amped-up state of tension and the urgency of their questions definitely put a strain on my fragile state of calm. I don't know how movie stars and politicians can stand that sort of attention all the time.

I could feel the little girl in me wanting to run away and hide up in the safety of that backyard tree and wait for this all to go away, but she was only a memory now. The only way I could send her any love was to do the sort of standing up now that I had never been able to do back then.

The thought of the bomber's close presence repulsed me, but I didn't fear that he could attack me or anyone else. This time the demon only existed in my mind. The shackled defendant hauled in for this trial was nothing more than a powerless captive.

Once we were inside, it took about an hour or so for the trial to get to me. I was one of the first witnesses to testify, and we all waited together in a tiny room right outside the courtroom. It wasn't much larger than a storage closet and was extremely hot and stuffy, a feeling emphasized by what we were getting ready to do.

The trial was closed to the public, leaving the reporters and media sitting to one side while the rest of the seating went to victims and their families. The judge had instructed the bailiffs to make sure any of the victims who wanted to attend got first choice on the limited seating. They also had an overflow room with video and audio, so no one missed anything.

About five minutes before I was to be called in, an agent came in to say that the stand was still pretty close to the defendant, and did I want to have it moved? I swallowed and told him not to bother. Asking for special protection from that man felt to me like giving him power he truly did not have.

I had come to a simple realization that there were two ways to look at this thing. One, I could wonder if he was far enough away for me to be safe, or two, I could ask why I should give *him* the comfort of having more distance from *me*. He was the one with something to fear this time. It was important to me to let him know I was not afraid of him.

I walked in wearing a dress short enough to give Felicia, my prosthesis, a full viewing. I kept my head up while I was sworn in, and I walked straight over to take my place on the stand. I later learned that certain reporters on Twitter said I walked with a slight limp. Maybe that was supposed to make me seem more sympathetic or something, but I can assure you it wasn't the case.

The questions were simple, all of them things I had been asked many times before. I doubt I was able to offer anything of value in proving the prosecutor's case, except to represent myself and Noah simply by being there. If that was all I did, it was good enough for me.

I've noticed that stage fright tends to go away once you start speaking and get involved with what you're doing, and I found that all the nerves I had built up dissolved while I was on the stand, although I couldn't help but cry when talking about my little boy's injuries. They kept me up there for less than half an hour, verifying photos, describing little details of what I had seen that day. There wasn't any drama to my testimony, and things were kept clinical and precise.

And then it was done. I heard, "Thank you, that is all, you may step down." The infamous Boston bomber never looked at me. Never met my eyes. Pretended not to see me.

That was fine, actually. Because I know for a fact that he heard me. Not only was the witness stand close enough for him to hear every word but I made it a point to speak clearly and in a strong voice. He heard me, all right.

My adrenaline carried me out of the courthouse, and Mom and I were soon back at the hotel. But once I was back in the room, I was completely drained. Who knew you could expend so much energy just keeping calm? I felt as if I had spent the morning walking a pack of very large dogs.

———

I think I left everything I had in the courtroom. But it still wasn't enough. Something didn't feel complete. My testimony was only one piece of a much larger strategy, and it hadn't offered any room for personal expression. *Just the facts, ma'am.*

And did I ever need to go beyond the plain facts. Many of us did. In response to any sympathetic social media version of that terrorist, or any other murderous attacker, we offered the shattered bones of dozens of innocents and blood pooled on the Boston streets.

In my heart I will always be grateful for Christ's mercy. He has stayed by my side and kept me strong, allowing me to remain a mother to my little boy and a member of a loving family, in spite of those two poisonous brothers and their lingering dark cloud. But I still hadn't said what I needed to say to this man.

So once in the hotel room, I went to my Facebook page and composed a letter to the surviving bomber. My intention was to cleanse myself of so many things I wanted to say or shout or scream at him.

As soon as I began to write, I felt a sense of quiet determination. I'm certain many hear about terror attacks, just as I do, and feel powerless to make a meaningful response. But like me, they also feel the need to hear truth spoken to the powers of hate. Indeed, as soon as I posted my letter, it seemed to touch a nerve with the public. I had hoped there would be others who took heart in it, but I didn't expect it to go viral the way it did.

My name is Rebekah Gregory. We don't really know each other and never will. But over the last two years, I have seen your face not only in pictures but in almost every one of my nightmares. Moments before the first blast, your stupid backpack even brushed up against my arm, but I doubt you remember because I am no one to you. A complete stranger. And although I was merely just a blip on your radar (someone that happened to be standing three feet from your designated "good spot" for a bomb), you have been so much more to me. Because you have undoubtedly been my source of fear since April 15th, 2013. (After all, you are one of the men responsible for nearly taking my child, and for the permanent image embedded in my brain of watching someone die.) Up until now, I have been truly scared of you and, because of this, fearful of everything else people might be capable of.

But today all that changed. Because this afternoon I got to walk into a courtroom and take my place at the witness stand, just a few feet away from where you were sitting. (I was WALKING. Did you get that?) And today I explained all the horrific details of how you changed my life to the people that literally hold YOURS in their hands. That's a little scary, right? And this afternoon before going in, I'm not going to lie . . . my palms were sweaty. And sitting up there talking to the prosecution did make me cry. But today, do you know what else happened? TODAY . . . I looked at you right in the face . . . and realized I wasn't afraid anymore. And today I realized that sitting across from you was somehow the crazy kind of step forward that I needed all along.

And I think that's the ironic thing that happens when someone intends something for evil. Because somehow, some way, it always ends up good. But you are a coward. A little boy who wouldn't even look me in the eyes to see that. Because you can't handle the fact that what you tried to destroy, you only made stronger. And if your eyes would've met mine for just one second, you would've also seen that what you "blew up" really did BLOW UP. Because now you have given me (and the other survivors) a tremendous platform to help others, and essentially do our parts in changing the world for the better.

So yes . . . you did take a part of me. Congratulations, you now have a leg up . . . literally. But in so many ways, you saved my life. Because now I am so much more appreciative of every new day I am given. And now I get to hug my son even tighter than before, blessed that he is THRIVING, despite everything that has happened.

So now . . . while you are sitting in solitary confinement (awaiting the verdict on your life), I will be actually ENJOY-ING everything this beautiful world has to offer. And guess what else? I will do so without fear . . . of YOU. Because now to me you're a nobody, and it is official that you have lost. I truly hope it was worth it.

Sincerely,

Someone you shouldn't have messed with.

I'm willing to admit to some anger there. But coming from the Obedient Preacher's Daughter, I can't tell you how liberating it was to speak my mind about this man and his attack. The little girl in me who would have wanted to run away or pretend there was nothing wrong needed to see the grown version of me stand up to this terrorist.

I can't prove that what I felt was truly righteous anger, but it certainly felt like it to me. I was angry on behalf of every human being placed at risk by those homemade bombs. I was even angry that I would never look at any stovetop pressure cooker the same way again, a simple object of domestic tranquility that had been transformed into a device of domestic terrorism.

The surviving Boston bomber was sentenced to death on May 15, 2015, but his formal sentencing hearing wasn't until June. As that date approached, the US Attorney's office called me again and asked me to prepare a victim impact statement. I agreed but let them know that part of my process of taking my life back and building a new normal that I can live with is to reject the role of victim.

I told them I would make a statement, all right, but I refused to come in and cry about what this had done to me. So I wrote a draft of what I had in mind and sent it to the US

Attorney's office for review. They okayed it, so it was back to Boston one more time.

This time my mom needed to stay home with my youngest sister, Allie, so I made the trip alone. Or I should say it was just me and Felicia. In Boston, I met up with two of my dearest former nurses, Naomi and Tracy. Naomi came and stayed with me at the hotel. I can tell you that even though I was prepared to be strong for this, it was so comforting to have a friendly hand extended that way. Naomi softened and humanized the visit and did a great job of giving me better things to talk about than terrorism.

The prosecutor had arranged for all the testifying blast victims to stay in the same hotel. A large group of us decided to have dinner together so we could get acquainted in a more comfortable environment than the courtroom. That turned out to be wise, but it was still the strangest kind of reunion I've ever seen.

The nature of the occasion had everyone in an especially kind and cooperative mood. We wanted to get through this necessary obligation as smoothly as we could. I believe we shared a greatly increased sense of empathy because of the evil that had done us so much harm. We called each other our "Boylston Street Family," and I came to be thankful for each one of us.

My heart went out the most to those who were there to speak because their loved one, whether a child or an adult, had been killed in the blast. Who can doubt that they felt, most deeply of all, the frustration of speaking out against evil that can't be undone on behalf of someone they'll never see again? What an awful thing for any parent to have to do, at any age.

Happily, when it came time to make the trip to court this time, I was mostly free of nervous anxiety. It was easier the second time, and in the hearing room I felt no intimidation whatsoever from the presence of the convicted killer.

Some of the impact statements were delivered by people who walked forward on prosthetic legs. Some were delivered by people whole of body but there to speak for the dead. It went on and on. The testimony was so raw and gut-wrenching that everyone in the courtroom paid rapt attention.

I was the last one called forward to speak, and I read the statement I had prepared. By this point I knew it well enough that I could have probably delivered it from memory, but I read it to be certain not to hesitate or fumble. Nothing I had to say was worthy of attention if I didn't maintain clarity.

I thanked the jury for performing their difficult job so well, then focused on the blank-faced killer in front of me. In that moment he made eye contact with me for the first time. Only now I stood unwavering, unlike the former Obedient Preacher's Daughter. Determination filled me.

People have commented that he looked like a lost boy, a waif who got in over his head. Such people see his blank face as a canvas on which they paint their own imaginings of who they think he is. Here is what I told him.

> I was asked to give a victim impact statement, but in order to do that I would have to be someone's victim, and I am definitely not one of yours or your brother's. For months now, everyone has watched you basically gawk at the horrific footage of the devastation that you caused, with little or no remorse. You even saw an up close video of my own legs completely blown apart. And I have to ask, did that make

you feel good? I can only hope it felt as good as the numerous operations we've all had as a result.

Each day you have spent the majority of your time in this courtroom fiddling with your pencil and cracking jokes with your attorney, while innocent people have had to come in and rehash the most heart-wrenching details of everything that was taken from them. I even witnessed your refusal to stand up and acknowledge the jury on the second day of the trial. Remember that aggressive nudge from Miriam? Yeah, I saw. As a matter of fact, it was very much like the one your backpack gave me the day of the bombing. And of course, if these were normal circumstances, I would simply ask if this was how your mama raised you . . . but that would be a whole different issue, now wouldn't it?

And I get the general idea of how these things are supposed to flow. But it is hard for me to wrap my head around spending my time talking about what you're already aware of. While it's absolutely important to explain the severe role PTSD plays in both mine and my child's life now, as well as the long-term headaches of being an amputee, what's more crucial to me is that before you die, you are shown a bigger picture of what your act of hate has truly done.

So in case it slipped your mind, I'm Rebekah. And since I was standing a couple feet away from the first bomb, your brother is actually the one who blew me up. But since he's not here, you get to be the one I give my dose of reality to. So listen closely.

Terrorists like you do two things in this world. One, they create mass destruction. But the second is quite interesting, because do you know what mass destruction really does? It brings people together.

Over the last two years, the other survivors and I have seen the hearts and souls of millions across the world. An outpouring of love that stretches hundreds of thousands of miles for one act of hate that stretched a couple hundred feet. And while you seem proud to be responsible for blowing up Marathon Monday, the legacies of Martin Richard, Lingzi Lu, Krystle Campbell, and Sean Collier blow up the entire nation EVERY day. Let that sink in for a minute.

Because when people look back on April 15, 2013, they won't remember your name or your brother's. Instead, what they will think about is the courage and bravery everyone has shown and the amazing feats those affected have gone on to do. Do you know how many foundations have been set up to give back and help others? And how many people have now made full-time careers of traveling the world speaking out against evil? That is why it is so funny to me that you smirk and flip off the camera, because truthfully I feel like that is what we are doing to YOU every day we continue to succeed, fake limbs or not.

And in preparing this, I asked my seven-year-old if he could say one thing to you, what it would be. His reply was better than I ever could have imagined: "You made us stronger."

So by all means, smile, gawk, make your jokes, and hate Americans. But when you are sitting in your prison cell, I want you to remember this one promise: I, Rebekah Gregory, vow with the rest of my life to use the platform I have been given to do my part in changing the world for the better. I will come up with new ways every day to shine my light brighter than the day before and continue to stress the importance of truly enjoying every minute we are given, no matter the circumstances. When I look down at my leg, I will not allow myself to become angry. Instead, I will count it as a blessing that I can try to encourage others through the hand that I have been dealt. And even during those frequent nights when

I wake up due to nightmares, I still will not hold any resentment. I will only let it give me further drive to keep pushing forward, no matter how many times life blows up in my face.

So despite what you think you have done, reality clearly states that you and your brother have lost. While your intention was to destroy America, what you have really accomplished is actually quite the opposite. You've unified us. And though we have a long way to go, because of such a horrific event, there are that many more people ready to do the dirty work of getting rid of evil once and for all.

I can't believe that you, at twenty-one years old, didn't think twice about wasting such a precious life, and I'm sad that you won't be here to see what happens next.

We are Boston Strong. We are America strong. And choosing to mess with us was a terrible idea. How's that for your "victim" impact statement?

Afterward, a US marshal who had observed the hearing from the packed overflow room told me that the crowd in there burst into a standing ovation when my statement concluded. He grinned from ear to ear and said (I'm paraphrasing to keep our family-friendly rating), "You sure told him." He also gave me his pin.

The judge's final remarks to the convict before rendering the sentence were eloquent. I particularly loved this part, and still do:

Whenever your name is mentioned, what will be remembered is the evil you have done. No one will remember that your teachers were fond of you. No one will mention that your friends found you funny and fun to be with. No one will say you were a talented athlete or that you displayed compassion in being a Best Buddy or that you showed more respect to your women friends than your male peers did. What will be remembered is that you murdered and maimed innocent people and that you did it willfully and intentionally. You did it on purpose.

You tried to justify it to yourself by redefining what it is to be an innocent person so that you could convince yourself that Martin Richard was not innocent, that Lingzi Lu was not innocent, and the same for Krystle Campbell and Sean Collier and, therefore, they could be, should be killed. It was a monstrous self-deception. To accomplish it, you had to redefine yourself as well. You had to forget your own humanity, the common humanity that you shared with your brother Martin and your sister Lingzi.

It appears that you and your brother both did so under the influence of the preaching of Anwar al-Awlaki and others like him. It is tragic, for your victims and now for you, that you succumbed to that diabolical siren song. Such men are not leaders but misleaders. They induced you not to a path to glory but to a judgment of condemnation.*

The surviving bomber, now facing death, began his wait in prison for his date with the executioner. He may have thought he would continue his jihad from behind bars, but his contact with the outside world has been hamstrung. No person other than precleared attorneys, paralegals, or investigators may participate in phone calls with him or even "listen or overhear" any part of the calls, which cannot be recorded.

His nonlegal mail, phone calls, and visits are restricted to immediate family members only. He can send only one letter

*Milton J. Valencia, "Judge Excoriates Tsarnaev before Imposing Death Sentence," *Boston Globe*, June 24, 2015, https://www.bostonglobe.com/metro/2015/06/24/judge-excoriates-tsarnaev-before-imposing-death-sentence/s4IVL9PTCeznIqEYcTuJMN/story.html.

of three double-sided pages to one adult per week. One adult can visit him at a time, but no physical contact is permitted.

Family members may not record phone calls with him or discuss the contents of their communication with any third party.

He is not allowed to talk to the media at all.

He can't share a cell, participate in a group prayer service, or communicate with any of the other inmates.

And while he waits, his outdoor access is limited to a small enclosure where he can see a patch of sky and little else.

———

I didn't travel to Boston for the sake of the sentencing. For me, the trial and sentencing were vital pieces of the three-dimensional puzzle I call my life and the process of taking my life back from the fools who tried to steal it.

*Part Six*

# WHERE *We* LANDED

# -17-

# When You Try to Stop Smiling and You Can't

Late in the summer of 2015, with the trial over and the sentencing done, my life came full circle in the form of an old boyfriend from my first year of college. Ten years earlier, Chris Varney had been a fellow student and resident in my dorm. Several girls on my floor and guys on his floor had formed close friendships with each other. It gave us a sense of family at a time when a lot of us were feeling far from home and intimidated about our futures. And right off the bat, there had been an unmistakable connection between Chris and me.

Back then, we had an easy dating life and our bond was deep. I always enjoyed his company and looked forward to hanging out with him and our mutual friends. He had been the first person, aside from my roommate, who I met at college. From day one, we were inseparable. We might have fallen into a much deeper relationship if we'd had the opportunity, but we never found out if anything more would develop between us.

During my second semester, my sister Lydia got sick. It was heart trouble, and it was giving her some of the symptoms of dropped blood pressure and dizziness I had experienced—in short, she began to struggle with the same POTS condition that had plagued my teen years. I soon decided the best thing to do was to move back close to home.

It was a bittersweet farewell with Chris and the others in my dorm. But they all understood my need to be close to family.

This happened before Facetime, and Skype was still brand-new and not widely used. There were certainly other ways to communicate, but we were all students and most of us were also working. Long-distance friendships are hard to sustain under a flurry of daily obligations, especially at age eighteen. And so I quickly lost touch with Chris and the others after moving away.

It was a happy surprise to reconnect with him on social media ten years later. I saw on his Facebook page that he was coming to Houston and reached out to him. He let me know his trip was job-related, but he was coming a few days early to hang out with his best friend, Nick, who also lived in Houston and had been one of our friends in college, and Nick's fiancée. He suggested we all meet up. I thought it sounded like fun to see Chris after all this time, and his visit happened to fall on a week when I was in town and my schedule was clear. That almost never happened at this extremely hectic time in my life. We made a date to meet with Nick and his fiancée two days later.

When the date was made, it was just old friends meeting up for dinner. I knew that what Chris and I had for that short time had been powerful, but it was such a long time ago and we were so young then. Still, I felt excited to see how he had turned out. One of the things that always impressed me about him was how considerate he was, a real Southern gentleman.

Later that same evening, I was lying on the couch talking with my girlfriend Rachel about all the craziness the last few years had brought. I swore I would never allow myself to get close to anyone else, and most certainly would never settle down. I was fine with it being just me and Noah forever. This went back to my promise to never allow another man to betray us, especially Noah. It's not that I had decided to hate men or turn against them; it was that no matter how well I performed in other areas of my life, I didn't trust my own ability to see a man for who he really was.

Sometimes it takes a friend to slap you just hard enough to hit your reset button. Rachel laughed at me and asked if I really planned to live life as a single mom, at the age of twenty-eight. I objected to the question. Noah and I could get along without a man, although it was easier on me than on Noah. I understood how much a boy needs a good father to help him define his own manhood.

But I also knew that no father at all was better than a toxic example of manhood who would cross a boy's wires and mess up his thinking with countless little bad examples. Noah had seen too much of that already.

Rachel was still unimpressed with my ability to maintain my solitude and raise my little boy and reminded me that even though it had been a long road, she still felt I deserved a good man and she didn't believe I would never find one.

She and her husband, Cody, had been by my side through my recovery, amputation, and divorce. If anyone knew me inside out, it was these two. A friendship like that doesn't come around often, and the fact that our sons were also close was icing on the cake.

I suppose that at this particular point in life my friendship with Rachel and Cody was the main reason I still believed in any lasting sort of love. The life they had built together was one to be admired and was as genuine as it comes. They were still in love after eight years and two kids, and I knew I had a lot to learn from them.

---

I agreed to meet Nick and his fiancée, Lauren, along with Chris at the restaurant Taste of Texas, which was owned by my gracious benefactors, the Hendees, and was also where we'd held the farewell party for my leg.

So I walked in and Chris was sitting there. It felt so good to see him again, and the way his face lit up when our eyes met was beautiful to see. He looked great, and once we began to talk and catch up, he was still his charming self. Before I knew it, the evening was moving right along, with everyone laughing and talking as if we did this every week.

This thing between my old college boyfriend and my ten-years-later self was unlike anything I had experienced. It felt crazy, but in the best of ways. And for me, there was a strange familiarity I had never experienced. Maybe if the term *déjà vu* could be used to refer to a person, that would capture it.

The best part of it, the most fun of all, was that whenever our eyes met while the others were talking, he beamed from ear to ear and I could tell that he couldn't stop himself. It was like seeing a grown man blush, just as charming as can be. He would just sit there grinning at me while Nick and Lauren talked, and neither of us could wipe the smile off our face. The spark between us was ridiculously strong.

I loved that he could be slightly self-conscious with me while also confident enough to make his feelings plain. He was just as I remembered him, but with another ten years of seasoning under his belt. And, of course, I was looking at him with different eyes than when I was in my late teens.

I already knew that Chris is a true gentleman of the South, from a good family with a loving mother and an openly affectionate father. Their faith is as important to their family as it is to mine. His Southern accent is deep, showing his background in coal country, but there is nothing rough about him. He is courteous and kind.

Our eye contact was electric. We probably didn't do a very good job of hiding it, but our friends were merciful and pretended not to notice (much). Our rapport was almost like telepathy. We started finishing each other's sentences— obnoxious stuff for outside observers but absolutely magical for us because Chris made it clear that he was smitten too.

Whenever I spoke, I could feel his concentration. He was glued to every word. It wasn't that I was saying anything important; it's that whatever I had to say was of interest to him because it mattered to me, and he was making that clear.

I felt so delighted and surprised by this little class reunion that I had to fight to avoid giggling like a happy moron and blowing milk out my nose. So much for my vow to live as a nun or whatever I'd had in mind.

By the next day, our new little group had planned another gathering. Not only was it great to catch up with my old friend Nick, along with seeing Chris again, but Lauren and I also clicked as if we had known each other for years.

The following night they all came over to my house for pizza and a movie. I introduced them to Noah. He usually took a long time to warm up to new people, yet he and Chris hit it off right away. I've heard so many horror stories about single men who can't handle dating a woman with children. But what I had missed so far was the realization that my mother's relationship was also with a man who had embraced her kids as his own, and it was not just the result of sheer chance. It was the result of loving, hard work. If it could be done once, it could be done again.

———

That night, after Noah went to bed, Chris held my hand for the first time. It was so electric that it's embarrassing to talk about it now. He let me know he wanted this relationship to grow. I know how corny it sounds, but at the same time I would wish for just such a corny experience for every one of you. Go ahead, when the moment comes, and grin ear to ear like a complete idiot. That's my advice. It feels great, and they can't arrest you for it.

Chris was still holding my hand when he turned to me and said, "Rebekah, you have no idea how much I loved you in college."

Who talks like that after two dates? Except it wasn't too soon; it was ten years in the making. The only thing new was our mutual realization of what we had almost lost years ago. We had sweated through long study sessions and laughed at lousy jokes and shared our early ideas about what we hoped to do with our lives.

Chris is smart, funny, sensitive, decent, and all the good things about being a Southern boy. I already knew so much about him. I knew how he behaved in the world and how he lived out his values. I knew he was level-headed and not impulsive. I also knew it was completely out of character for him to be so blunt and emotional, and I might have been concerned about it if the core truth wasn't already plain to both of us. It's just that he was the more impulsive one. Or maybe he was simply the braver one, for saying what we both were feeling.

So it turned out that my disappointment in the "dream marriage" and my frustration and embarrassment over the divorce were not going to guarantee a future of single motherhood. My painful previous experiences had yielded me at least a little wisdom, and under the power of that wisdom, every one of the carefully reasoned arguments I had built up in my mind for avoiding a new relationship dissolved.

After that, the more time we spent together, the more all the little pieces just kept falling into place. Later, when I got to know Chris's dad better, I saw how that man's strong emotional support of his son and his gentle, manly personality had combined to form Chris into a secure and well-loved son, and his mother had instilled a decency and respect in him that went to his core. In the years since I'd known him as a college student, he had grown into a stable and mature man.

Happily, Chris decided that he was moving to Houston. When his company opened a position for him in Houston—simply because he said he needed to be down here—we decided this was God's plan all along. Chris took every opportunity to show that his passion was not fleeting, and he made special effort to build a solid rapport with Noah.

As for my little boy, Noah took to Chris with a bond that was beautiful to see.

Now this new normal was more like it, when it comes to new normals. It was a *lot* more like it.

What a gift to be able to experience moments so sweet along with my little boy. Sometimes it makes me cry with gratitude. There is a minor miracle in being present in the world, together. You know that first warm day of spring, when you step outdoors and take in that first big breath of fresh air? That sense of gladness?

Noah and I kept right on discovering deeper ties to Chris, who wholeheartedly embraced both of us. Chris agreed with me about the importance of our spiritual lives, that it wasn't enough to go to church on Sunday and then spend the week caught up in the passions and distractions of the world. Can I tell you how good it felt to already know his family background and see his faith lived out throughout his life? In that home, religion is a connection to God, not a rack of judgment. Their commitment to following Jesus Christ mattered so much to me.

Chris and I both endeavored to find a model for our lives in the teachings of Jesus, understanding that we would fail, and fail often, but also knowing we would be far better for doing it.

He told me I was his "one that got away" and he wasn't going to let that happen again. For the actual proposal, Chris and Noah and I were all at his older sister Kristie's house in Cincinnati. His parents were also there, along with Kristie's husband, Jeremy, and their two kids.

I was starting to worry that Chris might eventually regret leaving his job and his birth family to move to Texas to be with me. This came out of those moments that replayed in my head of my biological dad saying I would never be good enough for anyone. But when I brought it up, Chris just looked at me, smiled, and shook his head like I was talking nonsense.

That evening I was watching TV with his parents when he called for me to come upstairs. When I got there, I saw him down on one knee, holding out the most beautiful ring. He said that he had wanted to plan something more elaborate, but after hearing the worry in my voice, he knew now was the perfect time.

That's one of the reasons I love Chris so much. He takes time to know and understand my heart. The moment was absolutely perfect, and the whole time he was down on one knee, his little niece Kortland (who was three at the time) was jumping all over us. All she knew was that something exciting was happening and she wanted to be smack in the middle of it. The whole thing was crazy and chaotic and that made it all the more special.

Afterward, Chris and I celebrated with his family. His sister did my hair and makeup and took engagement pictures, right then and there. It was intimate and wonderful and perfect. As for the wedding, I had never wanted a fancy ceremony. I was never one of those girls who had her wedding day planned out by the time she was ten.

So when Chris and I were making wedding plans, we decided what we really wanted was just the two of us. We went on a trip to Montego Bay, Jamaica, and got married there, four months after that first dinner. It was everything I could have wanted and more. Simple but elegant. There was a gazebo right on the water where the service was performed. The resort decorated it with beautiful tropical flowers from the island, and the ladies at the spa put some flowers in my hair and did my makeup.

When I walked out onto the beach and made my way down the pier to the floating gazebo, everything in my life suddenly made sense. This was the person I had first come to know and to love at the age of eighteen, and the one I know God intended for me.

We had a preacher from the island and two witnesses from the resort for the ceremony. Then we had dinner under the gazebo out in the middle of the ocean at sunset. After that, since my leg was really beginning to hurt, we had our first dance in the hotel room. Chris took off my prosthesis and picked me up and I danced on one leg. It was the best night of my life.

Back in Houston, we began our married lives. Both of us went back to work with the goal of getting a home that had enough space to grow our family but that was all on a single floor. I can maneuver stairs well enough with Felicia, but I can't wear her full time. It's much easier to roll around in a chair at home, which works until you hit a stairway. So flat is good.

Chris accompanied me on my speaking trips whenever he could get away. Not only was the aid and support appreciated but his presence always bolstered my morale. I felt then as I feel now: safe in his company.

That's what I would call a silver lining. You know the feeling. I wish everyone who reads this a generous helping of silver linings too.

Chris and I were together for a speaking event at a Presbyterian church that was far enough away to involve a plane ride, and we both had a deeply moving and delightful encounter with Julie, who was a runner and had been at the Boston Marathon with her husband on the day of the bombing. Julie volunteered to drive us to and from the airport, and it was so important to her to do this for us that she also brought her 2013 marathon medal and presented it to me. I was overwhelmed by her kindness.

Julie is a generation older than I am, and she and her husband had been married for decades. Julie was inspiring to us as a younger couple when she spoke of the living relationship she and her husband sustained. Even after so many years, they both still loved to put on music and dance in the kitchen.

She floored me with that. Really, can any marriage fail if the couple still dances in the kitchen no matter how long they've been married? I felt like I'd just climbed a mountain to enter a cave and receive a great truth from the monk who lived there. This athletic, big-hearted woman distilled a wealth of marriage advice and counseling down to a single thought: Can you dance in the kitchen together, week after week, year after year?

Noncoordinated people can relax; it doesn't matter whether you literally dance, of course, as long as there is something special for the two of you to do. Your kind of kitchen and your kind of floor, week after week, down through the years together.

We should all be so lucky. If we are not, then we should be so determined and do it anyway. Life goes by so quickly, whether we make brave choices or not. We get a few blinks of an eye and a half-dozen twirls in the sun.

Each tiny piece of shrapnel that is still embedded in me also left a slicing track through my flesh, leading up to its current resting place. In most cases, the blood vessels rerouted and the muscle tissue regrew. But damage to my internal organs was more of a problem. Before I left the hospital for the first time, my doctors had cautioned me, saying it was unlikely I would ever be able to conceive a child again. If I did become pregnant, they had no confidence that I would be able to carry the child to term.

That news was a tsunami. It was so overpowering in its scope that I didn't deal with it at all at the time. I was still bed-bound and rolling around with my leg elevated above my heart, feeling grateful for five minutes of Dangle Time. Childbirth is a nice dream for a healthy woman to have.

When I first got that news, I still had far to go before I could be called healthy, but I was hungry to bring a healthy woman back to this life of mine. So thoughts of childbirth got shelved. They joined those other concerns that nothing could be done about until I got on my feet, off the patient list, and back among the living.

Time went by. I got better. I learned how to use a prosthetic leg. I got strong enough inside to confront the bomber in court and at his sentencing. I fell in love and got married. I was healthy enough for us to make a home together.

And in that new home, Chris and I agreed that having a family together was so important to our picture of the future that we would adopt children if we couldn't have our own. We both realized that the only way to test the doctors' theory was to see if I could get pregnant at all. We understood the medical explanations behind their skepticism of my chances of bearing a child. And we had no argument to offer.

What we had was this: we were married and we loved each other so much that there was no way we could avoid seeing if, between my medical condition and the will of God, Chris and I would be allowed to bring a new life into the world.

# -18-

# Ryleigh Michelle and Noah Michael

Frankly, I had little hope of conceiving another child. It wasn't that the doctors crushed my hopes with their opinion as much as they confirmed what I already suspected. I didn't need to see the scans to know my body was still laced with shrapnel. I could visualize the slicing trails that all those pieces had made when they cut through me. How every piece managed to miss my vital organs is beyond me. The parts of me that took the worst impacts were parts I can survive without.

Nevertheless, while the shrapnel left enough of me to stitch back together, I could feel the odds against conceiving and they were embedded in my flesh. Even if my reproductive organs were undamaged, my immune system was already under constant strain from fighting the inflammation and infection from the embedded particles. The additional burden of pregnancy could prove to be too much, perhaps for both of us.

Chris and I talked it over and discussed all the possible outcomes, risks, and rewards if we could maneuver our way through this and make the right choices. And no matter how many times we went over it, we arrived at the same conclusion: We want a family. We want a family bigger than the three of us. All three of us have so much love to give to a fourth.

━━

We both strongly feel that it's part of our purpose in this life to build our own family on the principles our parents instilled in us. We both also want to make a solid contribution to the extended families we now share. That was how we got to the decision that if pregnancy wasn't in our cards, then adoption was the way to do it. We agreed that bringing up a young person by surrounding them with love and treating them with respect, while teaching them a solid moral center and holding to those expectations, was far more important than questioning the child's biology.

We agreed that while we wouldn't enlist the help of a fertility doctor, we weren't going to use birth control either. Instead we would go forward as a married couple who wanted a child and leave the rest up to God. Chris knew I harbored a secret fear that the bomb had taken my reproductive life away from me, but we both chose to ignore it. I think my fear was a strange sort of protective device, to ease the shock if my body failed me.

I didn't see clearly enough to ask myself why I still accepted a prognosis that had been made back when I was in the hospital, long before I had rebuilt my body in the gym and regained a lot of my strength.

I didn't feel frail anymore. The intense workout program had done its job on my overall musculature as well as my endurance level. But in spite of that, there had been so many major challenges in such a short time that I found myself braced for another calamity I would need to engage and overcome.

One symptom of PTSD that I didn't recognize at first was a faint sense of lingering dread. Do you know it? It hovers in the background and sounds a subtle but persistent warning, conveying the feeling that unless you're braced for the worst, you are going to take the blow unprepared.

I assume this was probably why, a few weeks into our new marriage, in spite of my joy over having this relationship to carry into the future, I found myself walking around with a light heart over our daily life but still feeling physically tired and vaguely ill. I didn't think much of it and sputtered along for another two months before I became frustrated enough to mention my symptoms to Chris.

He was protective and urged me to go see my doctor. While he hadn't been around during my postmarathon hospitalizations and the early recovery period, he knew enough about my medical condition to be convinced that any unusual symptoms needed to be checked out.

So: doctor's office visit, blood tests, a little waiting time . . . and the doctor came back with the verdict. "You don't feel ill because you're sick; you feel ill because you're pregnant."

You were ahead of me on that, right?

Yep. It's normal to feel queasy for the first trimester. And not only did I know that but these were also the same symptoms I'd experienced when I was pregnant with Noah. Proving the power of a good mental block, I went so far down the road of thinking that we could be wasting our time hoping to conceive a child that I didn't see my symptoms for what they were.

So mystery number one was solved: in spite of everything, I could still become pregnant. While that was great to know, the deeper question came next: Could this blasted and stitched body of mine carry this child long enough to give birth?

We went about life and this new pregnancy in a state of optimism, with no way to know if our child could make it through the goal posts with us but ready to seize any opportunity to help the baby do just that.

The first months of the pregnancy went by without any setbacks. I felt strong enough to carry my baby, and preliminary tests were all good. Eventually we saw the sonogram image of a girl. And at that moment, the daughter I had dreamed of pairing with big brother Noah officially entered our lives.

We started looking at girl names right away, and our favorite was Ryleigh. At first we didn't have a middle name for her. Then Chris called me one day from work to say he wanted her middle name to be Michelle, the same as mine. He made it clear this was really important to him, and I loved it. Noah's middle name, Michael, is the masculine version of Michelle, so now both my children would have my name in theirs and also have Chris's last name, Varney.

This was no longer idle speculation. Ryleigh Michelle was on her way. We were ecstatic, and Noah was delighted to know he would be a big brother at last. When we first announced it to him, he told us that he had been waiting for a sibling his whole life!

———

One ordinary Friday, with the due date still several months away, I developed sharp back pain. It started out kind of like a pulled muscle, that sort of thing. It was no big deal. But as the day wore on, the pain got worse.

I soon learned why my doctors had been so negative about my chances of carrying a child full-term. We went to the hospital when it became obvious that this wasn't going away, and when we arrived I was already beginning to dilate. This child was coming, and it was far too soon for a safe birth.

They gave me injections that were supposed to stop the labor. That worked temporarily, but then they discovered I was bleeding internally. Weakness soon came over me and I felt like I was fading out. My blood pressure, already low, began to fall to redline levels. My lungs were filling up with fluid from all the medicine they were having to pump into me to get Ryleigh's body as ready as possible to be born so soon.

My condition quickly degenerated to the point that there was concern for my life. I was put on oxygen, and they gave me one blood transfusion, then another. And soon after, we found out that I was suffering from a placenta abruption.

Everything just developed with such terrible speed, as if some giant jack-in-the-box had sprung open. Chris remained by my side as my advocate, and my dear mom and dad had to pace the floor once again and hope they wouldn't get a call saying that Ryleigh and I had lost the battle.

In spite of the blood transfusions, it was a struggle to re-place everything I was losing internally. We were so worried that it would be too late for our little Ryleigh by the time they finally stopped the bleeding, but miraculously she never went into distress throughout any of it. My body was the only one that was suffering.

They needed to give me a forty-eight-hour treatment of steroid shots, but the longer they kept her inside of me, the sicker I became. By Monday morning they had no choice but to go ahead and finish inducing labor. In spite of their earlier attempt to shut down the labor process, this baby was about to come, ready or not.

It became clear that I was going to have this baby the old-fashioned way, regardless of all the high-tech devices around me. There were several times throughout that weekend when doctors felt they might have to do an emergency C-section, but fortunately, when it came time, they said I could try pushing first. After all my blood loss, it was safer to do it that way than to risk more loss of blood with a C-section.

She was out in sixteen and a half minutes. The birth itself went well enough, and Ryleigh showed up as a living but astoundingly small version of a human being. She was fully formed but terribly underdeveloped, meaning she had the usual preemie problem of lungs that were not ready to support the breathing process. She had to have a breathing tube, feeding tubes, and two IV lines in her navel for additional injections.

Still, she was here. Whether our daughter's time in this life was to be long or painfully brief, we vowed to surround her with love during her stay. Little Ryleigh was so very tiny and fragile that even being held in my arms would be too much stimulation. She was still a creature of the womb, and her body wanted to be back there now, even though my body could no longer carry her.

And so there she was, so unequipped for life in this world of cold air and hard surfaces. At first we were allowed to lightly touch her, perhaps gently place our hand on her forehead, but the doctors quickly put a stop to all stimulation when her blood indicators began to drop. Her systems were underdeveloped. Any touch or stimulation, no matter how well-intended, took away energy she needed in her battle for life.

The first time I got to hold her was on Mother's Day weekend, six days after she was born. That was for only five minutes. The rest of the time she was in an incubator, with no sound or light disturbance and the constant administration of food and meds.

On the eighth day of her life, Ryleigh was placed in complete isolation, with a blanket over the top of her incubator to seal out the light. Introducing her to the world was not working well. The new plan was to re-create womblike conditions for our little girl in every possible way and hope she would be able to continue developing. The hospital reconfigured Ryleigh's little physical world as much as possible to make it vanish from her perception, returning her to a close approximation of the darkness and warmth of womb life.

In spite of all the tubes, we posted pictures of her online and asked for prayer warriors all over the world to step up for us. We had already seen what they had done for me during my own hospital stay, and only hoped that something miraculous could happen again with our precious baby girl.

We didn't ask for people to petition God to change his plans on our behalf. We simply asked for prayers directing strength to Ryleigh. *Please, Lord our God, allow our tiny daughter, Ryleigh, to draw a good breath, and then another, and then another. Allow her heart to beat strong in her chest.*

We who are broken, we who are filled with flaws, we who sometimes seem to resist the better parts of our nature for no reason but human stubbornness, nevertheless become forces to reckon with when we humbly join hands and hearts. In our limited human way, like a series of batteries that each hold a tiny charge but together can deliver lightning, we call down the great reservoir of God's healing force.

I will never have words of greater thanks, greater awestruck gratitude, than when I tell you we watched Ryleigh begin to improve. Doctors were hopeful but puzzled; she was too premature and too underdeveloped to thrive, yet she began to do just that.

The breathing tube was switched out for a less invasive CPAP breathing device, and after a couple more days they were able to remove that too. We were overjoyed, even though it didn't appear to make medical sense. Ryleigh was months away from her due date. Her lungs shouldn't have been able to take over the way they did, but we watched it happen before our eyes.

We posted more pictures of her and received massive outpourings of loving support and kindness. Even those who don't believe prayer can help others at a great distance could see how much all the expressions of love and concern sustained me. That also went for Chris, our parents, and all the doctors and nurses who made it their business to give this girl a chance at life. It was a tonic for the spirit to gladden the heart.

Many parents know that waiting for a child to recover is the same as waiting on your own recovery. Everything else stops except for this one life. All distractions of the world fall away in importance. They exist all around but without connection to you.

Chris spent most of his time at the hospital with me, but whenever he had to go deal with other things, I sat next to Ryleigh's crib. There was nothing to do but wait and watch. The old demon of helplessness tiptoed into the room and took a seat next to me. What a sterling job this demon does in the way it uses frustration and despair to isolate us from God and from our confidence in God's plan for us.

The helplessness was as familiar as an old friend and as ugly as an old bully. It conjured up all my past fears and my loathing of being caught in another disastrous situation where the deepest concerns in this life are threatened but where I can have little or no effect on the outcome. Who doesn't hate that?

The first two weeks of Ryleigh's touch-and-go life were an emotional roller coaster, but my little family was able to pull together through it, and in the long run I think we can't ask for much more. We don't seek to be spared life's troubles; we seek to rise through them with our faith intact.

Since the wonderful company Chris worked for allowed him to take time off, not only was I spared his absence at a time when I needed him so much but we were also able to keep more of a balance in our time with Noah as well as with Ryleigh. Noah had been so patient and supportive, especially for such a young boy, and it was important to keep him in the loop and in our immediate concerns. Noah's own relatively positive experience with the hospitals in Houston and Boston, and his observations of how the doctors helped my recovery, gave him the tools he needed to stay positive amid all the trauma.

We were at the hospital from morning until night, and I usually went home around ten o'clock each evening. Some nights we couldn't bring ourselves to leave. Chris and I sat with Noah and ate takeout meals outside Ryleigh's room, even when we couldn't do anything to help her. There was no way we could walk off and leave her to fight for life all alone.

We were also able to have some ordinary bonding time with Noah because of the extraordinary care of our nurses. Not only were they completely skilled in their care efforts but they were also exemplary in their compassion toward us and toward Ryleigh. As my nurses in Boston had done for me, these people clearly made it their personal mission to give this little girl her best chance at life.

You recall those important five minutes of Dangle Time each day when my leg and foot sutures were new? Even such great elation and relief paled next to the technicolor joy of being allowed to hold Ryleigh on Mother's Day for that same five-minute time span. She had been kept alive by our genius doctors and highly skilled nurses, and I also believe the intercession of our blessed prayer warriors helped her remain in this world with us. The medical odds appeared stacked against her on every front, for a while there, but she did not decline. Instead Ryleigh began gaining strength.

Throughout this time, Noah's patience was tested. But he showed the ability to understand that our focus had to be on Ryleigh for now. He was already looking ahead to being a big brother. Our shared experience in recovery had put him on board with this in a manner I would expect from a grown man.

In such moments, I saw that Noah's sense of the preciousness of life had been amplified by the Boston experience. I made it a point to tell him how proud I was of him, and I could see that it mattered to him to hear that. If we could get Ryleigh well enough to come home with us, she was going to have a great older brother to show her the ropes.

At last, fully three weeks after Ryleigh's birth, the doctors changed her ICU status to "feeder-grower." Can I tell you how welcome those two words were to us? Our tiny preemie, fighting for life since her first breath, was feeding and growing instead of fading away, having gained over a pound. It's a huge distinction for a preemie to reach that stage, because the physical functions of sucking, swallowing, and breathing are the hardest for the premature human body to get going. The difficulties can combine to cause a failure to thrive.

One doctor spoke of the "lightbulb moment" they often see in those preemies who manage to make it out of the ICU and begin to eat without the help of a feeding tube. At a certain point the struggling little body appears to just fire up, like a light coming on. A flare of energy rises in the child, and this new life begins to thrive.

And so Ryleigh joined in with all of the other new feeder-growers in the world who were being cared for at that moment. They may not have had time to get organized yet, but they were already busy composing the next generation. For her, and for all of them, the light was on. This world's air, light, and food had only made her falter, not fall. My family will always be grateful for the kindness, the compassion, and the attentive energy of all those who prayed for Ryleigh. Your testimony exists in her presence here.

Finally, we began getting ready to take her home.

Her last test before being officially released was for our little family to all stay together overnight in the hospital's transition room. Ryleigh's vital signs remained stable and her little light never flickered. She was ready to give it a try with her people, at home.

———

Okay, maybe this is a coincidence, and maybe it's not. Ryleigh was in the hospital for twenty-six days: the number of miles in a marathon. It represented everything we want for her: stamina and perseverance. We took it as Ryleigh's personal announcement of determination, coming from a very small flame who refused to go out.

# Conclusion

## *Happy Continuations*

I began this book by describing my story as a spiritual journey. This story traces the growth and development of one struggling soul. In describing where I have come from and where I yet hope to go, I am determined to walk the journey of a Christian woman in America, where not only our faith but also the values supporting that faith are under heavy and persistent attack.

Human nature being what it is, we are a mix of good and bad, and everyone around us is too. No matter what church we join, we find ourselves surrounded by the walking wounded.

There have always been pretenders whose faith was no reflection of their identity behind closed doors. And people of faith are under attack from both unbelievers outside the church and hypocrites within the community.

One valuable lesson I have managed to learn is to forget the dream of a happy ending. We focus too much on happy endings. Why focus on what ends? In our house these days, we go for happy continuations.

When my spirits are low, I am still capable of doubting everything I do. It is then that my relationship with Christ calls me back to the things that matter most in my life and always will, no matter what: being a mom to my son and daughter, a loving wife to my husband, and an active member of my family. The stability I find there centers me in the greater stability of the Lord. It's my skeleton, holding me up.

I don't hear an audible voice speaking to me in answer to my prayers, like you might in a Hollywood movie. Nevertheless, I feel a silent pull: strong, compelling as gravity itself. It keeps me focused when I would otherwise be lost. God doesn't solve problems for me like a magical servant. What he does is far greater. He puts strength back into my legs when they would otherwise fail me. He deflects despair. He protects me from the terrors of struggling alone. He shows me a smoother path.

So a bomb explodes and changes your life. Simply by taking place, the event serves as a stark reminder of the ticking clock we all carry. My story, and your story if this book speaks to you, is one of a spiritual arc, extending over time. These arcs stretch from wherever each life begins to wherever it will end. All along each arc, strength rises and falls with the challenges that lead us either closer to Christ or away from him. We each have our own story. We can choose our reactions to daily challenges, but they will never stop coming.

For me, as one Christian woman, mother, and wife, neither the extreme conformity of OPD nor the clench of internal stress can consume me if I pull my fears out of the way and allow that space to be filled with God's love. Of course, distractions are always present. I don't have any special method for dealing with them other than to stop myself as soon as I notice that I'm off course and then reset my personal focus. I pray for patience and for strength and suit up to play again. Rinse and repeat.

People ask me what my secret is. Anyone who tries to follow Jesus already knows that "the secret" isn't a piece of information. It's *trust*. It's trusting that God has control. It's growing in my faith even as I face obstacles. It's asking myself how Jesus would ask me to look at life.

As a Christian, I believe this perspective is available to anyone who seeks it. It will filter out all of the distractions and guide our journey to becoming the person God wants us to be. There is no secret to it.

I got to this point in life by the power of the Holy Spirit and after being forced to learn how to care for myself in spite of an inner narrative that assured me of failure. Repairing my body wouldn't have had much point if my spirit couldn't have thrived. The power of Christ alone sustained my strength. It enabled me to do my best in situations when I otherwise would have fallen down.

Today, when I meet people who tell me about feeling various forms of darkness in their lives, I focus on asking what is covering their light. Sometimes that darkness can remind us to tend to our souls. If we do that with conviction, the truth we share will resonate with others, perhaps many others.

As for life's misfortunes, I don't look to my relationship with Christ to keep misfortune away or to protect me from tragedy above anyone else. But I have already found, so many times, that this thing we Christians call *salvation* allows me peaceful confidence. We stand assured of love and existence beyond the physical limits of our lives. The more I pray on that, the less compulsive I feel.

———

When I speak of taking my life back, I am not referring to a specific end point. The end of this book is not the ending of my story, and my journey isn't over. It's just that I have this uncovered light, now, because I see the effects of its presence all through my journey of recovery.

I wonder if it's the same "lightbulb moment" as when life flares in a struggling premature baby. The light calls to me. My ambition is to share it to the great benefit of others.

I clearly understand how much has been done for me and my family by kind people who also allow that light to guide them. When we look back at the people in our lives who did or said things that truly stuck with us in Christlike ways, my experience is that these are moments when they were letting their inner lights shine.

We keep one another afloat with moments of rejoicing. Fellowship can take place in a passing exchange between strangers just as well as in a hall full of the faithful. For me, that goal is the bull's-eye of my personal target: live today and each day as a happy continuation. The light that guides me is the simple secret to how I took my life back.

I wish nothing less for you.

# Acknowledgments

**From Rebekah**

When I was ten years old, I made myself a promise that by my thirtieth birthday I would write a book and have it published. Writing has always been my outlet, even from a young age. Of course, back then I didn't have the slightest clue what it took to actually write a book, let alone the process for it to appear on bookstore shelves.

Now that promise has been made a reality, and there are so many people to thank for making it possible. So in no particular order, here we go. Thank you to:

My parents. It has been a long, hard road, and both of you have stuck by my side through everything. I hope that by doing this I have made you proud. That is all I have ever set out to do, even though I have failed at it many times. Thank you for your unconditional love and for instilling in me God's love and faithfulness.

My husband, Christopher Keith. Without your unwavering support I never would have had the courage to finish this book. You keep me going daily, and I am so proud to be your wife. Thank you for rescuing me from myself and showing me the greatest love I have ever known. I feel so blessed to have the opportunity to share this life with you and raise our precious family together. Forever and nothing less, my babe. I can promise you that.

Noah Michael and Ryleigh Michelle. Being your mom is the greatest title I could ever have. I hope that as you grow, both of you will know, without a doubt, how much I love you. At very young ages, each of you has already proven how much fight you have. My hope is that this fight will only grow stronger with every obstacle you face. No matter what, I will always be your biggest cheerleader and am so excited to see the plans God has in store for your futures.

Author Michele McPhee. You encouraged me to take this journey, and without the push I never would have done it. Thank you from the bottom of my heart for your help and your friendship.

Anthony Flacco. Throughout this process, you have become more than a coauthor. You have become my friend. Thank you for every exhausting hour spent together translating my story into these beautiful chapters. You have made my biggest dream come true, and there are no words to describe what that truly means to me.

Sharlene Martin of Martin Literary Management. You're so much more to me than a manager. Thank you for seeing more in me than I see in myself most days and for pushing me further than I ever knew I could be pushed. This has been one of the most rewarding experiences I have ever had, and I owe it all to you for taking a chance on a Texas girl and her dream.

Editor Vicki Crumpton, Twila Bennett, Lindsey Spoolstra, and the Revell publishing team. I knew from our first phone call that, if the opportunity presented itself, you guys were the only team I wanted to work with on this project. It has proven to be one of the best decisions I have ever made. Thank you for believing in my dream enough to turn it into a reality and for every moment of this amazing adventure.

My sisters, Hannah, Lydia, and Allie Grace. You three will never comprehend how much I love you and how proud I am to be your sister.

My friends Megan Bugle, Lauren Schaefer, Karah Clark, Rachel and Cody Crosland, Lisa and Eric Lindley, Nick and Lauren Longo, Melissa Rainer, Naomi Stone, Tracy Kiss, and Helen Breyan. You all keep me going on a daily basis, and my life is better with each of you in it.

My second parents, Edd and Nina Hendee. There are no words to describe how grateful I am to know both of you. We became family the day we visited for the first time, and I can't imagine life any other way.

My fellow Boston bombing survivors—I am so proud of each one of you who continue to pick up the pieces to your own lives every day. Never stop fighting.

The doctors, nurses, and medical staff who have been involved in not only my care but also my children's over the last several years.

Stephen Plant and Cesar Soto with Orthotic & Prosthetic Associates. (You both have become family, and Felicia wouldn't be a part of my life if it wasn't for you guys!)

Each person who donated to The One Fund and my outrageous stack of medical bills!

My prayer warriors and supporters from around the world.

And finally, every single person who risked their life to save ours on April 15, 2013.

These are the people I continue to take my life back for every single day.

Thank you. Thank you. Thank you.

## From Anthony

I am grateful for having had the opportunity to tell Rebekah's story and to acquaint readers with her lovely personality and her depth of spiritual devotion. The challenge of maintaining one's personal faith in the face of terrible and destructive events is one that defeats the efforts of so many beleaguered people. Although Rebekah has traveled through many of the same dark corridors, her faith has sustained her and proven its worth. It is my strongest hope for the readers of this book that they will take strength from her story and that it will help sustain them when the inevitable catastrophes of life befall them.

I thank Revell for their faith in this story, and Revell editor Vicki Crumpton for her exceptional work, done with equal doses of talent and sensitivity. And, as always, my gratitude goes out to Sharlene Martin of Martin Literary Management for her superlative efforts in getting this story out to the world.

Rebekah Gregory is a woman and mother whose life was forever changed due to the bombing at the Boston Marathon on April 15, 2013. This act of terrorism may have claimed her leg but it could not claim her spirit. She is now a powerful motivational speaker who encourages people all across the country with her message of faith and hope. She lives in Houston, Texas, with her son, daughter, and college-sweetheart-turned-husband.

Anthony Flacco is a *New York Times* and international bestselling author of ten books by major publishers, which have garnered multiple awards. He has a master's degree in screenwriting from the American Film Institute and lives in Seattle, Washington, with his family. His nonfiction book *Impossible Odds* is in development at Warner Brothers Studios for a feature film.

# *Rebekah's* ANGELS

On April 15, 2013, my life took an unexpected turn when my five-year-old son, Noah, and I became survivors of the Boston Marathon Bombing. Right before the blast, I made the decision to sit Noah on my feet, fearing that he might otherwise get lost in the crowd. That spur-of-the-moment decision would ultimately save his life. Thankfully, Noah was able to walk away with only a few minor injuries. It is my belief that angels were all around us in those moments and that both of our lives were spared for a bigger purpose.

Because of the support Noah and I received from millions of earthly angels around the world, Rebekah's Angels was founded. This foundation will provide resources and funding to children suffering from PTSD (posttraumatic stress disorder) due to trauma. Children may suffer from PTSD after experiencing acts of violence, injury, or an accident on many different levels.

As with Noah, the emotional aftermath for children can be far worse than the physical trial. Fortunately, with proper treatment children who are treated early following a traumatic experience will be less likely to exhibit symptoms of PTSD later on in life. This has become one of my greatest passions in life—to provide a way for families to get the help they need for their hurting children. It is vital for their future.

For more information on how to help Rebekah's Angels, go to www.rebekahsangels.org.

# Meet
# REBEKAH GREGORY!

For information on how to request Rebekah for a
speaking engagement, please contact Premier Speakers
at www.premierespeakers.com/rebekah-gregory.